# Spells

## 21st-Century Occult Poetry

*edited by*

Sarah Shin and Rebecca Tamás

# Contents

# The Broken Open

> Magic exists in most societies in one way or another, and one of the forms it exists in a lot of places is, if you know a thing's true name, you have power over the thing, or the person. And of course it's irresistible because I'm a writer. I use words, and knowing the names of things is – I do magic, I do make up things that didn't exist before by naming them.
>
> Ursula K. Le Guin, *Worlds of Ursula K. Le Guin* (dir. Arwen Curry, 2018)

In the beginning was the Word.

No.

This is about the moment before the word, when everything inside you is broken open.

Words, together; multiple and multivalent, coming in a rush, sounding in a chorus, a force like a waterfall. A dam breaking. A difficult birth.

*

The word 'witch' enters written English in c.890, according to the Oxford English Dictionary, to mean a man practising sorcery ('wicca', weak masculine). It is another hundred years before it is used – in writing – with its more familiar gendered dimension: witch from 'wicce' (feminine). Where does it come from? Old English *wiccian*, from the German *wicken*, *wikken*. 'Of obscure origin.'

Obscure origins are, often, in an undocumentable language spoken, down the generations, far from the privilege of writing. In *wikken* we can perhaps hear a whisper of the German word *wissen*, knowledge; *wikken* might indicate an alternate form of knowing, one given into earth and heard in the sky.

Khairani Barokka writes backwards and forwards from this difficult birth, of the knowledge birthed in its difficulty, in her spell-poem:

> Chani knows the term is archaic, gives its history
> for mystifying chart, points to femmeness and creative wombs
> broken, bust open, diminished. Disrespected, pushed,
> slapped red to know one's place by muscly hands.

To know one's place becomes a profound art, in the broken open. It takes this density of words, their history.

This isn't about God making the world with the Word. It's about the witches who've been remaking the world, unmaking the mess he made, ever since that difficult birth.

*

To be a witch, then, is to know words. To be a witch is to know, in your bones (your tired bones), where the word 'witch' might come from. Birth stories, origin myths, are wandering and plural, partial but yours. Not someone else's definition of your self, but what you have learned through dangers untold and hardships unnumbered. The thing you have to tell, have to say.

Listen to Canisia Lubrin sing of the origins and the journey in 'Geology Lesson 4':

*she just them bones she was born with,*
*is all* she'll take with her burning
a dominion of horns and spell
books, and seven recited rants,

How to take everything it takes (with you when you leave). How to work the 'and' between books and rants, the written and the sung. How to spell it, over and over again, until it is heard.

*

It's irresistible, as the great mage Ursula K. Le Guin, who appears herein in the guise of one of her last poems, says. To conjure with words, with the right words, as editors Sarah Shin and Rebecca Tamás write:

> Spells are poems; poetry is spelling. Spell-poems are vehicles of change that take us beyond the borders of the rational into a place where the right words can influence the universe.

Summoning hexes and feminism for *Spells*, they called (for writers and voices from) the four corners and six directions, in recognition of a 'pluralistic magical language' that provides 'sacred spaces away from everyday experience of violence and harassment.' Not an escape, but 'a space for healing and liberation', working on the physical body, the affective body, the thinking body, and the subtle body of the spirit. Spells to call these four bodies together, against a world that pushes them apart and fractures them. Spells for what has been broken, open.

* * *

And then we are in the open. It is an enchanted space.

Let us revive, in the English language, the tradition of being enchanted when we meet each other. *Enchanté/e, encantadx*, that charmed greeting in French or Spanish. Let us delink it from the tired old rituals of courtship and make it anew, the sign of witch meeting witch.

Let us mean it. Let us mean the enchantment of taking care, which is where writing and magic meet: care that begins in the right words for things, in the chant that sings in *enchanted*. What poetry can do if we let it – take care of us.

Enchanted to be here. Only such spells as Shin and Tamás are capable of working could bring us together – and make no mistake, it is work to summon and enfold such jostling, dancing, protesting, loving spirits. Across the time and space of silencing, of fear, of separation, of loss, we have come together. Make no mistake: when we encounter such voices – feminist, queer, decolonial, dis/abled – there is magic at play beyond even the ordinary, practical magic of writing and publishing, the dilation of time and instant connections between writer and reader.

Be gentle, take care with these words as the writers have taken care with them. Take the care they offer you in their chant, their rhythms and movement, their caress of the surface of language. To stand with us in this circle with its centre everywhere and its circumference now/here is to be under a spell. A pleasure to meet you here: enchanted.

Enchantment is vulnerable. Vulnerability is enchantment. Enchantment, like vulnerability, is necessary.

We are living in the broken open. So much has piled on to us that we push back. The crush is so intense that we cry out.

We are open: we are broken.

*

Hoa Nguyen opens her spell-poem with an immediate invocation of the real violence that has broken us open. If we accept the power of words, then we feel the stabs in our bodies:

> Mouth wet with life
> & stabbed
>         Stabbed and staggered
>           three times of knives
>
> as three literal people
>
>         stab me      metaphorically
>           in Greenbelt Maryland

Trauma remains in the body – the mind-body. It could be said that trauma, painfully, reveals that body is also mind, affect, spirit; that all four meet at the point of the knives. This is not to endorse the violence, but to mark how far we have come from living in our multiple, attuned bodies.

Trauma is, in or behind many of these spells, the broken open: the realisation of how great is the need to find the right words to record and to transform; how great is the power inside us, the power that the violence comes to steal and erase.

*

That anything of what could broadly be called witchcraft survives – other than what was said of it by inquisitors and torturers – is evidence that it works; that it continues to conjure and enchant, even when suppressed. We could say it survived by hiding, but that's only partially true. It survived in the broken open, in the wounds of trauma, as memory does. It survived by arising at need, and by being difficult: localised, specific, demanding, resistant, persistent. In repetitions and in the echoes of rituals.

In '1947: Spell to Reverse a Line', Bhanu Kapil calls us with a simple ritual, to make a place to meet; the place where the sum total of the world that makes the poet was broken open, the place of Partition and great pain:

> If the line is a border and a border is a boundary award.
>
> If you left at night.
>
> If you were warned by your neighbours.
>
> If you saw through a hole in the cart...
>
> And if this glimpse repeated on loop, a story of early childhood woven into bed-time fairy-tales and stories.
>
> Then this is a spell to reverse the line, the hole, the night itself.

Witchcraft – like the violence it opposes – works by repetition, by the looping and looping and looping of a thread, by the network of words. Kapil's line is a reminder that textiles and text are connected. Textiles, historically the preserve of women, predate architecture. The loom was the first computer. Plaids may encode calendars. The first clay figurines found in Turkey and the Balkans wear fringed kilts whose knots, like the Quechua *quipu* or *khipu*, may be records, journals, messages – or spells.

Recording history is, after all, itself a spell. Knotting, stitching, and weaving are enduring metaphors for how poems, in particular, work themselves. Kapil shows us the underside of the cloth, the work, where the process and the programme become one and we see the trace of the body doing (or undoing) itself. As Bones Tan Jones offers in a fire-cider spell for strength, 'self-defence is more than a punch to the face or a kick in the groin: it is a holistic practice that exists in the many ways we go about our days, navigating our lives and boundaries.' It is a practice; that is, something we have to do, and do again, not as an accretion but as finding the root. Radical self-love.

*

Moving only at their own pace, spell-poems do not just record history, but reorder it, reorganise it into new lines that reveal the obscured. They change time, reminding us of the phrase 'for a spell.' Poems slow us down, dance us to their rhythm, turn time from a line to a circle.

Or a prism; refracting their thoughts through elemental crystals. Francesca Lisette sees, through rose quartz, the facet of time that ritual seeks; its specificity and singularity vibrating outwards ad infinitum:

> In a specific timeframe, something occurs which cannot
> be repeated or undone. Each reading is a ritual. It is also a
> performance. It is also a gift.
>
> Because the body is more than a frame. It is a vibration.

Where does a spell begin and end? What do its effects look like if we move in the time of poetry, that long cycle that stretches back into 'obscure origins' and forward into transformative resurgence? What if we come to our elemental selves of earth, air, fire, and water (in the European tradition), to the vibrations that make volcanoes and waves, gentle breezes and earthquakes.

If a spell is a crystal, it holds compacted, geological time. Lisette's spell-poem asks: How can such vast histories be made to reverberate? How can the traumatic memories of their formation be released, with a healing scintillance?

*

Words, like crystals – like water – hold a density of memory that detonates inside us. Erica Scourti's spell-poem 'Lost to the Phosphorus' tests spit and Smart Water to see if these liquids can hold the two languages, two alphabets, of their fluid-filled body, 'sweat and salt', English and Greek, together. 'What are your symptoms?' they are asked, and so asks us. Scourti re-sounds the Mediterranean origins of English words, a reminder that here is linked to there. We are inextricable. Words bind us, together.

And where do we go from there? Scourti concludes:

> I'm no good at endings- too prone to clichés-
> because kaimos, then metaphrasetai-
> but I wanted you to come away with something
> to hold
> a protective shell,
> glowing in a sweaty palm
> a skinful reminder

The shell is in your hand, they say. Listen. Sing.

*

Magic comes down the line: feel the sweet frisson, the freight of responsibility. The right words are imbued with power by the righteousness of those who spoke them before us. We sing humbly to continue their great songs.

Through the lines of this spell-book, we raise a chorus for Audre Lorde, lifelong activist, writer, and speaker of secret truths to power, who wrote of a singular bus journey in her memoir *Zami: A New Spelling of My Name*:

> the angelic orchestration swelled, filling my head with the sharpness and precision of the words; the music was like a surge of strength. It felt rich with hope and a promise of life – more importantly, a new way through or beyond pain.
>
> I'll die this death on Calvary
> ain't
> gonna
> die
> no
> more!
>
> The physical realities of the dingy bus slid away from me. I suddenly stood upon a hill in the center of an unknown country, hearing the sky fill with a new spelling of my own name.

Lorde offers us a map to that unknown country and a grimoire of its potencies. They are not easy to access – Lorde did not rest. She rode the bus, and wrote poetry there, turning the great wisdom she learned, through struggle, into words we can all read. And by reading, open our ears to that angelic orchestration: that's the magic.

*

Lorde's teaching of radical self-love is founded upon a spell, the original spell: to say your name, magically, and make your true identity.

Karen McCarthy Woolf names one version of herself in 'If I Were a Buddhist I'd Chant for Your Happiness':

> I shall propagate Sea Wolfes and watch
> them shoot into my own army of glittering
> green gargoyles.

Woolf/Wolfe: the flexibility of English, which crackles with homonyms and homophones, with centuries and continents shaping diverse orthographies, a reminder that what is written is an echo of what is spoken or sung – a 'glittering' shape on a page that binds the voice into a spell.

*

Reader, say to the poets you are meeting here, in Tai Shani's prayer from her work *My Bodily Remains*, 'When we say love we say that we see you for who you really are, we say that I am brimming with unassigned faith, that I am also collecting the precious pieces.' You are collecting these precious pieces.

What a spell creates, as you speak it, is you: a sense of your power to create. A spell spells you. Jen Calleja ends her spell-poem with this crucial instruction:

> You just have to mean it
>
> and when I say mean it
>
> I mean: your intention must always be to save your own life.

Read all these words aloud, together, and mean them. Give that gift to the writers who crafted them, and the editors who bound them. Search out more of their work, invoke them in conversation and in your own writing and singing.

Break open the walls, the distance between writer and reader by taking the words into your body, your history. Let them break you open as, together, we enter this unknown country, this decentred centre, this intention to save our lives.

Please, be enchanted. It could save us.

*

I do magic, Le Guin says, simple as elemental.

In their spell-poem, CAConrad says:

> poetry is the opposite of escape
> but makes this world endurable
> how the smallest puddle
> reflects the entire sky

These are the stakes of re-enchantment: the smallest puddle, the entire sky. The relation between each individual being and the ecosystem that we all contain, breathing it, swallowing it. In Conrad's practice of (Soma)tic Rituals, poetry is exactly the opposite of escape because we are doing poetry (or doing magic) the entire time that we have, and live in, a body.

Poetry, or magic, takes charge of intention: of how our name is said, how our bones are held, how we breathe, how we see. It means believing in ourselves: conjuring the belief that our intentions, our actions, matter – not because we are special or gifted, but because here we are, in the world and part of it.

As Conrad continues:

> everything matters because everything
> hurts someone somewhere as it is mattering
> we became all we carried into the mast
> migratory patterns given to the love again

The '-ing' of the present participle weaves a 'migratory pattern': changing time from a past to which we consign wrongs, to a continuous present (in Gertrude Stein's phrase) in which 'it is mattering' and we have to attend.

Repetition matters, as it did when we were children, chanting and singing. Do it again: that's what ritual means. Repeat and repeat until it is in your bones. Read this book in order, then read it by chance, by procedure, by contingence, until it has you by heart, and you can go on.

'Repeat as many times as you like', as Alexis Pauline Gumbs ends-without-end her 'Love Spell for the Night of the Full Moon'. The moon cycles, Audre Lorde's poems persist, and the spell invites us to consult them as oracular. Each time we look up at the sky and down at her sister on the page, we renew, re-cycle.

Re-peat, as in: dig in, lay down, touch earth, transform through loss and grief.

'Everything / hurts' across the line break, but we keep (s)inging. If we attend, if we intend, it is the repetition, the ongoingness, that breaks us open.

*

Everything
hurts.

And yet.

That is what the magic says. Everything hurts and yet these words clean the wound. Words that will come to you when you are riding the bus, when you are holding a shell, when you are walking a line; when you realise that each of these seemingly ordinary moments can break you open; and in the break, these words arise.

'Rise up in the smoke of the palo santo', Le Guin spells in 'Come to Dust'. Poetry is the opposite of an escape: it gives us a place to be, where we are (doing) magic, because we endure.

> All earth's dust
> has been life, held soul, is holy.

Hold soul, as these words do, when everything / hurts. The memory of earth, in our mouths. In the beginning was, and is, just this.

*So Mayer*

# Prayer

*Kaveh Akbar*

again I am thinking of self-love    filled with self-love    the stomach
of the girl who ate only hair was filled with hair    they cut
it out when she died    it formed a mould of her stomach    reducing
a life to its most grotesque artifact    my gurgling internal devotion
to myself    a jaw half-formed    there are words
I will not say    the muscle of my face smeared
with clay    I am more than the worry I make    I choose
my words carefully    we now know some angels are more terrifying
than others    our enemies are replaceable    the stones behind their teeth
glow in moonlight    compared to even a small star
the moon is tiny    it is not God but the flower behind God I treasure

# Banshee

*Rachael Allen*

He'll sit in the window
at an innocent date
with wandering hands
over a port-green stool.
There's the kitchen
where I was murdered
where I was delivered
into a weapon with force
like a small model forester
axing up plastic logs
in a red wooden clock
murdered by a man
the sanctity of communion
I was never alone
the heavy smell of blood
misted up past the crockery
and the murdered girls before me
gathered up in plain cotton
the scores of my limbs
and the nub of my treatment
my hair was a clotted
pattern of wallpaper
like a tapestry of rabbits
and we left with my body
but do not forgive

so easily as that.
Tonight I laugh walking
towards his dark house
my head's a dun lantern
with split ends uplifted
my hands are barbed knots
to take it back
for I'm fury with a shell
and I'm petty.
The old boundary walls
where I leaned in the summer
swaying in my peripherals.
I don now a gray sheet
the dusk colour of bonbons
too seem more like a haunting
light pools through the mock-glass
and the door he approaches
the red door approaches

# Augury

*Nuar Alsadir*

The crow knows,
hangs under the sky
with accusatory inflection.

Wit gathers
and is gone to me:
I grow spectral, imitate stone.

Smoke rises
from the mission next door.
A man without a cup paces, starves.

# What Chani Nicholas Told Me

*Khairani Barokka*

The morning my mother gave up
on coaxing me out of her vagina,
after nearly two days, consented
to being cut open, I was born in a placement
speaking to difficulty:
            *'under the sun's beams'*.

I plucked hymns from wading
in the warmth, amniotic sea.
And no one was bearing me out
            unless my home was sliced in two.

How I see Chani:
Astrologer bursting sun from her bare bones.
Human and emailing to help with a Moon course.
            I don't crush a lot (just a player).

The stars when I emerged:
Close to the sun.
Venus retrograde, in Aries, twelfth house.
I hear from Chani *Difficulties*. Here: *Fallen woman*.
Chani knows the term is archaic, gives its history
for mystifying chart, points to femmeness and creative wombs
broken, bust open, diminished. Disrespected, pushed,
            slapped red to know one's place by muscly hands.

I know, Chani, yeah.
Read me like the salvaged medusa of nerves
            my body has become.

She speaks of my birth placement as archetype:
Venus conjunct Sun, retrograde heart of second planet—
*'In the myth of Inanna, this is when she dies*
*in the underworld*
            *and is reborn.'*

Sometimes the river with its faint whiff of tombs,
hand in its water, laughing back at abled prisons.
Coming into a thirty-third year of survivorship,
counting from when they slit my belly-sky roof
and placed my heart like an offering—
to burn under Sun's beams, ripping the empyrean,
befitting an epidermal ceiling.
            I'd wanted to stay.

My orbit of all things rebirths itself;
Chani tells me how, but I am ready, and already:
Firmament-heavy. Beaming back at the burning gaseous.
Mouth trying to be kind, fingers grasping
from all my house placements, Taurus rising half-dead,
half-scorned, half-electric, the bull a symbol
of my mother's Minang house, our clan house
back in the Tanah Datar village, its roof shaped as horns.
My belly-sky.

# Canopy

## *Emily Berry*

The weather was inside.

The branches trembled over the glass as if to apologise; then they thumped and they came in.

And the trees shook everything off until they were bare and clean. They held on to the ground with their long feet and leant into the gale and back again.

This was their way with the wind.

They flung us down and flailed above us with their visions and their pale tree light.

I think they were telling us to survive. That's what a leaf feels like anyway. We lay under their great awry display and they tattooed us with light.

They got inside us and made us speak; I said my first word in their language: 'canopy'.

I was crying and it felt like I was feeding. Be my mother, I said to the trees, in the language of trees, which can't be transcribed, and they shook their hair back, and they bent low with their many arms, and they looked into my eyes as only trees can look into the eyes of a person, they touched me with the rain on their fingers till I was all droplets, till I was a mist, and they said they would.

# golem

## *A.K. Blakemore*

you tell them not to fuck with you but they'll fuck with you
anyway maybe even fuck you if they can to give you a real reason
to steep your ear in breath they use to fashion some

apology out of a professed attraction to 'difficult' women –

Cleopatra was a cunt for going quietly –
carried out by eunuchs to feel the soft rain on her skin.

go down to the river and make a man with your bare beautiful
hands and knowledge of sacred geometry.

ensoul.
make him a mouth and spit in it.
learn the only boy worth trusting is your rabbi.

# The Gift

*Jen Calleja*

I was born with a gift
passed down from the sirens on my father's side,
the banshee on my mother's:
the protective charm of song.

Once, when only a child,
I made a woman weep from my singing.
My throat closed up not long after that
from a particularly ruthless curse.

Some years ago, at the moment of my certain suffocation,
and not without an amount of effort,
I managed to whisper a lullaby to myself
and it soothed my nerves and body: every knot unravelled,
        I became a river.
I knew then it would always be my greatest source of power

I can increase my potency by sipping on
honey    lemon    hot water
oily black coffee
gaseous black tea
*cortado,* water of the coconut
by sucking on
a salt tablet        a birthstone        a lozenge
by snacking on

creamed opals
topped with a trickle of gems: shards of
*citrine, aventurine, tourmaline, almandine*
negating the produce of the cow, the goat, the sheep.

Even at my most lacklustre I am better than men.
They think it's all about the words –
that mouthing or howling or pronouncing them is enough.

Casting occurs in the space where body and song harmonise.

The catalyst is sincerity, and sincerity requires no specific tone or
volume.

You just have to mean it

and when I say mean it

I mean: your intention must always be to save your own life.

# *from* Blackbox Testing

*Anthony V. Capildeo*

If ever I moved to London, it would be for the Thames (not for you (or you (or you (or a job)))).
Sweet (filthy (historical)) oculus.
Light arrives as the daytime allowance expires. Night arrives, like the deity dreamers require.
If ~ (Whose angel sucks fire-lozenges (in the silence of candle-compliant stone (amidst the memorial complaints of sailors (bruising erasure of cargo)))) If ever ~ (Whose shallows are the dickens) If ever I moved ~ (Whose dome whispers how roses glow alongside sunsetting Deptford pinks (multibranch cyclops showing floribundant (carnation coronations (dogs with eyes the size of hollow crowns)))) Moved ~ (Whose black depths cradle (graves (expel (the living)))) For the Thames ~ (I said this would not take long (but it is (would be) for the Thames)).

Given the chance ~ it skips ~ its spring ~ & enters autumn ~ What skips? ~ It ~ It ~ the best ~ translation can do ~ It ~ the dream ~ language ~ gestured ~ Skips ~ spring ~ Enters autumn ~ The sea is warm, the earth is warm. The air bites its own tail ~ Ouroboros breeze in an apple tree, the offputting air ~ n'a rien à dire ~ nothing, you say? ~ Felt want. Night. Ask. I do not ~ speak to thee. ~ Self-want. Night ~ take thy obscureness: ~ task ~ not ~ ask ~ Night runs consonants to vowels ~ starts the infinite ~ applies day as a finish ~ Stop ~ thy thoughts ~ are ~ donne ~ Summer was dormancy ~ summer as a farmer's town green dream ~ two peacocks flying ~ away to fly back multiplied ~ The painter painting ~ one peacock over & over ~ aspects ~ iridescence ~ oil ~ mirrors ~ Autumn tanks ~ Autumn's thankless ~ asks for night ~ dreams ~ with winter ~ I asked night for a wreath of winter ~ Night ~ feathered a woolf ~ waymarked a mansfield ~ for how far ~ below sea level ~ vowels ~ classed as afloat ~ owlcall ~ pleasecomeflying ~ submerged ~

Memory's exiled engineer deposited years of thoughts in horse-chestnut leaves on Magdalen Bridge that they might fall into traffic & water & light & wheel back again (just one more thing (emerald hedgehog egg-bearer) and another thing (magnolia's rival (candelabra)), like any memory whose (constancy is inconsistency (constancy is ingathering)) constancy is outpouring (tu joues? (toujours)), so in this way I dropped something into the Thames (je ne joue pas), or so I told it (un jour), so I told it I dropped it (on ne jouera plus), and as I dropped it (I swear) the Thames told me (it told me so) *je vous le jure...*

# umbra

*Elinor Cleghorn*

the skin belt holds faster than the bodice.

nightly, the cycle tightens        her whip hand over the whip man

        she was sure the pelt felt smoother in her dreams.

she'll make her journey later; her gallows-tree geography,

claws scored across the lines her mother drew.

*

back then, they called her the living angel; strange spectacle    so full of light and very feminine;

cynosure of men's coined eyes and grasping hands*

                (*please refrain from touching the exhibit.)

But her fingers blistered with cunning.

she cricked her joints    *click-click*    *and for my next trick*
    micro-flick

her reach    steradian    her resonance    an orbital thrum

forced stimulation        sounds grim in dark weather.

        her belly swelled round something darker still.

crawling like the dogs        she wrested bolt from latch and
hastened     heel to heel

no time. the waning sliver could betray her and crack the dawn
wide-open.

too long a subtle body        too flimsy too filmy

*lumen* he'd called her. *lumen.*     *mine my light mine my entoptic*
*seraph my saccade siren my mine remember I made you all by*
*myself out of rods and cones and I can slam the lid tight shut*

*whenever I like –*        *and babes, there'd be nothing left of*
*you.*

*

born *en caul*        born in the waters        never was much of a
swimmer that one, but no matter;

she made a little liquid breather.

for nesting purposes, a blanket bog sufficed        wetland mire
for a bright mare

wait:        this is where they harvest the electric

keep still or you'll blow a fuse        and pulverise surprise
surprise
the unexpected hits you between the eyes.

nine days her rising time        nursed herself on milkweed
bridled at her mother's bit.

blasted forth in the middle of the prisoner's cinema double-feature;

mere spent illusion. but lustre is a mineral thing;     Hygeia's dust,
a particular sort of promise.

she grew obscurer, hide-bound, laguno thickened bristles
prickles
contra her mother,          that nebulous princess,
          afterimage scorching the slick sheath of the eye-ball.

more moons passed. now she bore a dusky pelage.          it was
quite the wild shroud.
her baby guard-hairs shimmered     but this she kept a secret.
*and no-body knew she was there*

*

night is the shifter's magistrate.     but here we slink above the law.
our ministry governed by the loom-knot the stave the pierced
poppet
the *gala* songs          our call to roam

the others simply wear the skin          but mine is all epithelial.
self-cloak cellular          collagen basket-weave

look closer:          etched into the hem-lock there's a waveform
sawtooth
mother-tongue transmission
          (an echo only I can hear)

Come the morning I'll clothe it;        feed the children sweep
the front steps

bless the reverend

        but for these few hours our labours must remain invisible

our closeness to the earth is altogether necessary

with soil in our mouths we incant throat music        the glug and
growl makes angels of us all.

They fear our hunger; but we don't need men's blood        we're
smooth-tonged,

inclined toward a different kind of appetite.

the moon is limpid now.

I, born of light and its opposite, will lick my wounds in private.

# Camisado

*CAConrad*

after breaking in
the wolf
calmed
the hens
so he could
take his time with them
twists them open until the right
amount of memory fits into the song
another high price for belonging
poetry is the opposite of escape
but makes this world endurable
how the smallest puddle
reflects the entire sky
a return to every dream
our minds talked us out of
trusting our math of the star
your hand around my shoulder
poet astronaut you know I love you
I have no sense of failure when I am with you
everything matters because everything
hurts someone somewhere as it is mattering
we became all we carried into the mast
migratory patterns given to the love again
a way to end this secrecy of suffering
cut a door in the wolf so we
can retrieve our dead for
a world that matters

# Multi/direction Bio/poetics

*Nia Davies*

What I desired was to join the historic cult of poet-lovers. I would welcome any emperor the tarot foretold. Em*pourer* who comes unelected, who comes as my equal and ruler.

Can I sit you all around me in a circle on a black cloth? Arcane in saliva, your oils are already food for my lungs and can I breath in your discourse? You can all come and touch my solar plexus.

I tried keeping a film of many eyes, many gazes. Kept his smell on the pillow for three days. After the second it went stale. Some licked ears, others anus. Their differing Lacania. I would keep record of a person's constituent auras and vibrations.

But one cannot idealise difference forever before, well, difference. I overboiled with interaction. Laid down. One held my cheeks for years.

You've troubled this conversation into being, I thought, you've taken a beer blonde with my thigh. Can I slit the black cloth we're sitting on and put you in my orbit?

I had strayed into a mania of teeth. Also, a theatre of fluids. Theatre of intersecting narcissisms, poet juice, Bollywood yearning. The saints, my friends, billowing. Their discourse settling in the back of my action.

I tried to answer the questions they asked me truthfully but the voices rang out in their special timbres all container, no content. I tried to let myself contract. Now I lie in a darkened room to become less stimulated.

The word I learnt on this day was 'Scotchie'. So I thought of scotch tape sticky at our borders. Hey, come to the borderlands with me, a friend said.

I corresponded with this ruby counsel who took it to heart. Remembered the word 'metrosexual'. I anointed my bed to change its marital status. The reading rooms glowed with wheat and soil colours.

He asked to be smacked expecting I would choose the right side, but I took the left. I worry that's the wrong hand to take around here. Are you ready? The way to take poetry seriously is you can all come and pull up my cervical spine.

I've noted my flaws, they are hollows in my attention. And when asked, I visualised the multitasking demon, its shaky head and gripping claws. Then, later, the disintegrating owl demon, its grey feather dandruff. There is also the one who cannot give love, it pulls down in a glaucous streak through the organs, hampers the stomach. These all have their constituent allies ready to pull us back in an upwards motion.

But you need to be ready to be pulled up like that. You need to spell some aura of hello helo. Some of these bus journeys are not appropriate for filing invoices, answering emails. Sometimes men read your love letters over your elbows. Others ask you what you are writing becausc it is so unusual to see a person writing letters on to paper. Or even reading; a man approached me at the carousel to tell me he loved the fact I was reading a book and not a phone like everyone else and I'm staying at the Hotel Trident.

Other men have cared. Other men were 'splaining but I love my father too much to tell them to go. Others yet say they have a scotchie which means they have a woman they have marked as theirs somehow. I still don't understand the meaning of Scotchie.

Which of your demons or allies flushed up to the surface of this spell? Dearest, history surfaces in the blood that colours our lips. I wondered if I should feel all the unfelt shame of the ones who had come from my place before me. Or perhaps it's not possible to carry someone else's unfelt shame. Just the demons wriggling underneath. My love, the worst demon is the one who doesn't love at all. Its colour is slate.

# Ritual for Rose

*Paige Emery*

Preliminary conditions include: to be still, still to be open, open
to be able to sense, sense to allow nonthinking, nonthinking
to unpredict the future, unpredict the future to break open the
horizon line. Lie underneath Rose in the space between here
and  there (the space between here  and  there
is one of dreaming).

Find one Rose for infusing and one Rose for offering
Open by drinking Rose tea in stillness
Allow the perfume to open your heart like a flower,
here you can let down your thorns
and then have the right thorns  at the right time,
Finding love through the grief by being love
Ask Rose to teach you what beauty really  is
and how to walk in beauty.
Bring the other Rose to a creek, river, or ocean mother,
Sing into the petals of the Rose,  asking for love to stream.
Song is a communal language,  the Earth hears songs
Offer the Rose-song into the moving water, this gesture is
alchemical,
for love to stream.

# Bark!

## *Livia Franchini*

> *The business of selling illusions is – wouldn't you say? – a business that targets vulnerable people.*
>
> *You think so? You really think so, don't you?* [a pause] *Then tell me: who, exactly, are these vulnerable people?*
>
> Wanna Marchi, in conversation with Francesca Leosini,
> 'Io sono Vanna Marchi', *Storie Maledette* (Rai3, 2003)

Red mould grew in the tracks of the tiling at the summerhouse
    out of drains
like a clown ghost a bright blood it could follow us around
    sometimes
a whole afternoon in the heat slide the hem of your vest off one
    shoulder
or pool salted water in the dent on your lip those days a small
    distraction
could cost you your fingers permanently stained with the juice of
    some fruit

Illumination seemed to be ubiquitous those days certainly for a
    few years of this

our late childhood in spite of the fact we were growing fast in spite of
moving light from the T.V. to which we composed the number of the witch
telemarketing corsets fortunate numbers we were daring each other to listen
to the phone ring three times say each other's name three times in the mirror

Magic came to us then in short spells from a faraway channel thumbs swiped
on a forehead a cross salt stirred into a glass cup unbroken eye contact visible sweat
on the edge of a bright flame fingertips dipped in the soft wax of candles at dinner
of the red hair of the T.V. presenter her voice the same polish of dark ficus leaves
dragged face down on a stone floor the damp outline of a body on the pavement

You could always remember all the names of the capitals reluctant to drop
the habit of listing them one after the other unprompted the gall of it
she'd been giving us over and over the digits that made up the number yet
sitting at the adult table that night you seemed to have forgotten
the numbers counting down from a hundred the exact parameters of it

our available magic

# Love Spell for a Night of the Full Moon

*Alexis Pauline Gumbs*

1. Find the moon.
2. Ask yourself: how can I love myself deeper, more fully, more completely than I ever have before? And then find it: what is the shift you are ready for?
3. In the name of that shift, ask a new question.
4. Choose a letter of the alphabet that goes with your question (e.g. for a question about trust choose 'T')
5. Consult the concordance. If the letter of the alphabet you chose has a corresponding Audre Lorde oracle poem, read the poem three times looking in a mirror or directly at the moon.
6. If the letter of the alphabet does not have a poem, write a poem using only words that start with that letter of the alphabet. And then read it three times in the mirror or directly at the moon.
7. If you are brave, repeat the process asking yourself how can I love _______ (someone other than yourself) deeper, more fully, more completely than I ever have before.
8. Repeat as many times as you like.

# Lorde Concordance on a Night of a Full Moon

## *Distilled by Alexis Pauline Gumbs*

**From Audre Lorde's 'On a night of the full moon', originally published in *Cables to Rage***

**A**
a
and
am
as
as
as
against
again

and
against
at
and
attended

**B**
body
birds
between
before

be
beckoning
breaking
beaching

**C**
comes
curve
conceive
curving
come

**D**
darkly
delightful

**E**
eye
eyes

**F**
full
flesh
for
fits
flesh
frank
flesh
feel

flesh
forgotten

**G**

**H**
hungers
hand

hold
heart's
hands
high
hungers

**I**
I
I
in
in
I
I
inside

**J**
judging

**K**
knows

**L**
lips
limes

**M**
moon
my
my
mouth
my
my
my
my
me
moon

moon
my
moon

**N**
night

**O**
on
of
out
of
of
of

over
over

**P**
passing

**Q**
quick

**R**
reason
reservations
risen
roundness

**S**
shape
seeking
sunlight
sweet
sharp
skin's
stomach

spoken
speaks

**T**
the
that
that
the
the
thighs
the
taste
thus
together

the
thought
tide
the
the

**U**
under

**V**

**W**
waiting
warm
wanes
we

would

**X**

**Y**
your
your
your
young
your
you
your

your

your
your
you
your

**Z**

# The Hanged Man

*Will Harris*

He bought a seeded loaf and two ripe and ready avocados
and left them in the hallway, and at lunch the next day went
to Chipotle on Charing Cross Road, then back to work,

and afterwards bought his dad a ring doughnut from Tesco
because there were no jam doughnuts.

That night, though he didn't think he was a hoarder,
he started ordering records online and soon he had collected
the whole of Bruce Springsteen's back catalogue.

*I hate Bruce Springsteen*, he thought. *I want to eat better.*

The next week, listening to *Human Touch*, he dozed
and woke to find himself floating two feet off the ground.

Hanging there. His parents were alive and dead.
If only he could keep completely still he could remain
unscattered, forever on the edge of rain.

# FULL MOON LEECH PARTY

*Caspar Heinemann*

what is going on and why is it eating everything – are you
succulent, pig?
i snarl-want geodesic dome austerity, the austerity of sacred
geometry, fear
of the seeping night, fucking up upwards, another finger. not this
austerity
of domesticity's sandwich spread bright dull markt salmon,
literally dead but
worse still – actually dead. I tear off my top layer of skin to
practice tanning
animal hides so I can make myself a winter jacket myself out of
myself
fuck u capitalism, who's laughing now? me
because i can build a fire to roast chestnuts and
warm my hands but you
don't even have hands.
people are not made of bricks, they're mostly made of systems,
my drag
persona is called Nature.
luckily there is no crime anymore then
but for now i spend my time under
ground searching for the early warning signs
of sinkholes i might cover in green ribbons, moss and build
homes inside like everyone's arms that have ever been
a small architecture of warm blood

i am wearing a terror halo that burns when i feel
fear, so we can find each other glowing in the tunnels
there's no curse to cast, just a protection charm
PROTECTION AND ALL THAT IT IMPLIES
if it implies what it could imply, well.

my eyeballs are so heavy in their sockets, they're in my throat and
    i can't swallow / come
closer and read me your truth movement, i can lick your
    turmeric stains, grimoire or
stick some parts of some concepts to my skin like leeches
                i hate the ideology of the belief of the system of
                bricks of people who declare that
                bloodletting has no proven medicinal benefit
                but now i am sitting in a bath covered in
                feasting leeches
                and i don't even have the words to thank them
                for their labour

# *from* The Hermit

*Lucy Ives*

78.

A white home, mint mansard, ivy browning on a trellis. Shade in foreground. Branches pendant with parasitic vines. Now we are inside. A tan mother is here in a navy blazer. She pours vodka from a frosted bottle into a tumbler near her cereal bowl. She has been eating while standing.

On TV: footage of a slaughtered body. A gurney bears it away.

A teenage girl approaches from the stairs. She wears pale pink. She's sickening in her youth, mouth an overripe strawberry and big, plain teeth.

The mother's hand, with costume jewelry, slaps the TV off. The mother draws her shoulders together. She doesn't want the girl to leave.

The girl holds an orange backpack.

The mother pecks the girl's cheek, her fingers on her daughter's face.

It's very bright and now on the street the girl walks with a blue purse and orange backpack.

Before a Spanish colonial garage she pauses. Across the street is a man in sunglasses and a suit. Is he an agent of the law? The girl looks away, then back, but the man is gone. Breeze tousles things. The girl, staring, is seized from behind by a dark-haired boy. He drags her down an embankment hitherto imperceptible. 'You were screaming like crazy,' the girl says. 'The door was locked from your side,' she tells him.

A police officer appears. He holds a long black pistol. There is a chase. The boy is cornered by squad cars and subdued. The girl retreats. The officer with the pistol is her father.

Now we are in English class. There is floating yellow and/or turquoise light. Maps are everywhere. The girl is here. Someone stands at the front of the class and reads with a fat tongue. Now the murder victim in her translucent duffel beckons, and black liquid is in a pool. Human blood so plentiful that it is black. (I saw a sight like this on the floor of the subway once, years before I met you.) Quote: 'I could be bounded in a nutshell and count myself a king of infinite space, were it not that I have bad dreams.'

# to purge the desire to write like a man

*Rebecca May Johnson*

enter the archive
it is your body
remember
                    it is
                    a great many things
                    will become

enter the kitchen
you will find
your body
                    it is
                    a genius
                    will wield
a sharp knife
a shallow pan
a wooden spoon
a fitting apron
                    to make
                    tomato sauce*

put on the apron

skin and slice two white garlic cloves
open one tin of ripe red tomatoes
reserve six tablespoons of green olive oil

add the cold green oil
to the cold shallow pan
with the white sliced garlic
apply a gentle heat

and when
            the slices begin to dance
and when
            the perfume enters your nose
add the tomatoes

shake the pan a little only
a slight bubble
should bubble through now
simmer gently
for twenty minutes

do not stir

turn off the heat
add a caution of salt
stir and taste
add your palate's satisfaction of salt
stir and taste

you are ready

***found incantation*** **

now I no longer wanted to write like a man
because I had had children
and

I thought I knew a great many things
about tomato sauce
and

even if I didn't put them in my story it helped my vocation
that I knew them

* Adapted *Sugo fresco di pomodoro* by Marcella Hazan via Ruth Rogers

**Natalia Ginzburg, *The Little Virtues,* trans. Dick Davis

# 1947: Spell to Reverse a Line

*Bhanu Kapil*

If the line is a border and a border is a boundary award.

If you left at night.

If you were warned by your neighbours.

If you saw through a hole in the cart…

And if this glimpse repeated on loop, a story of early childhood woven into bed-time fairy-tales and stories.

Then this is a spell to reverse the line, the hole, the night itself.

No.

This is a spell to stop the loop.

To regain one's wholeness as a human being.

This is a spell:

My mother glimpsed, through a hole in the cart's soft wall…

1947: Partition.

By some estimates, 2 million people died in the transition of Muslim and Hindu populations from one province to another.

'I saw women, tied to the trees, their stomachs cut out.'

The image: partial, glimpsed, and it was only when I grew older that I encountered other models of working with language and imagery that were less to do with the value poetry places on repetition or recursion than an idea about expanding the image environment itself.

As if the image was the concentrated fluid.

Used to titrate.

Social medicines.

Or memory.

Because it was as if.

When my family crossed that line.

That border, that boundary.

That nothing more could be recalled.

That the memories of the train pulling in, its floor ankle high with blood and every person on the train.

Slaughtered.

Except for my uncle, who had been hiding in the bathroom.

Returned, intact.

To the speaker.

Exhausting the speaker to such a degree.

Forever.

Indeed, when I sit down to write, I also feel exhausted.

I blank out.

As I do when someone tells me they love me.

Yes, and what about this numbness, which I conceal from others?

Is it a trait?

Is inherited trauma like the water passed from one generation to another, placed in the hands of each person in turn?

But if the glass is broken.

If even one drop is spilled.

You will be punished so severely you will not be able to leave your home for many days.

Years.

Yes.

I lived in a family of people who survived a massacre or witnessed its aftermath.

They spent seven nights on a railway platform 'with dead bodies all around'.

My mother wept, telling this story.

To my son.

In a Mexican restaurant on Eisenhower Avenue.

It was my mistake.

He was writing a paper on colonisation. I said:

'Ask your grandmother. She's sitting right in front of you. She lived…'

Through these things.

'They…'

When I was a child, I lived with a mother who was still traumatised.

By these experiences.

Did her way of seeing the world.

Or recollecting it.

Cast a spell on my own brain?

The way that everything I wrote returned.

To the image of a woman's body.

Poked, upright or inverted.

Or pinned to a tree in the world.

I wrote about the neighbourhood of immigrants and workers I grew up in, on the outskirts of London where the Nestle factory drops its lilac skirt into the canal.

I wrote about patriarchy as something that happens outside the home but also inside it.

One night, I left England, unable to move from image to narrative in ways that were recognised as writing, at that time, by others.

But now.

Here I am!

So far from home!

Unable to write.

What I came here to write.

Convinced that if I could.

Then I would be free.

Of the extreme suppression.

That has shown up in all areas of my life.

How the indigo of childhood.

Its smudges and illegible writing.

Became my art.

This is a specific spell:

Catch a train from Amritsar to Lahore.

From India, that is.

To Pakistan.

To the city your family were living in.

Or vice versa.

When the neighbours warned them one night to go.

*Leave now.*

Before sunrise.

Did your grandfather burn his notebooks, scraping the ash into a tiny lacquered box?

My spell is this:

Disembark when the train stops.

Catch a taxi to the street where a house once was.

In a nearby café, order a freezing cold coffee.

Or chai.

And drink it, as slowly as you possibly can, savoring each sip.

In a place nobody spoke about or wanted to speak about.

Because it no longer existed.

Yes, relax.

Here, where everyone walking by.

Looks just like you.

Yes.

I have the strange feeling that if I could make this journey.

I could reverse.

The effects of a long-held suffering in my family system that makes its face known in the arguments of elders over property or ownership, but also domestic violence towards women and girls in its many forms.

Who was responsible for the suffering of your mother?

I remember writing that question in my notebook when I got to the U.S.

Because I wanted to write.

Because what will others inherit from me?

I am writing this spell for:

Other women or non-binary folks.

In the Punjabi Diaspora.

But also.

I want to make this spell open to others.

And not limit it.

To the loss, grief and hope that has marked my own life.

I want to open this spell or offer it.

To anyone who needs it.

To anyone whose family system or nervous system.

Has been marked by a war.

That preceded their life span.

And it goes without saying.

That you don't have to go there.

That you don't need a visa or cash or a ticket.

To cast this spell.

You can travel.

To these places.

In your dreams.

In your extreme way of making art.

In what it is to be with others.

In the way that you are with others.

Here.

Forever.

Now.

# My narrative costume is a witch without reputation

*Amy Key*

Sometimes I imagine the sea as a cauldron
I am making spells in

~

There is nothing more
pleasurable to me
than my ardent unavailability

~

My hate is plaque
intractable & on my teeth

~

When I wake up my skin
is like polystyrene
someone's dug their nails into

~

Meanness
making a home of me

~

If you need me I am

rethreading the pearls
of my reproach

~

*I have created a difficulty for myself*

~

They asked about my *Baby Plans*
[how do you feel about dying?]

~

My uterus is an idyll
where forgetting happens

~

Certainties are limpets smashed from rock
with rock

~

I survived without birthday candles, so can you

~

I had to lie early to account for things I knew
I had to talk
I had to lie

~

If you need me
allow me to press all my worries
against you like a hot flannel

~

Together let us figure out how to live
through our failure

~

You there! Stop composing your riposte!

# Incantation against Mumsnet (JFGI)

*Daisy Lafarge*

**SIOB**

FWIW, SWOI MMTI

OTOH OTOH OTOH

WB, EWCM

OW OW OW POAS!

OW OW OW POAS!

& DH POAS!

AIBU? AIBU? AIBU?

*YABU </3 YABU </3 YANBU <3*

PFB: PITA

D&V, DTD

SIL TTC RF, WWYD?

'YABOS' 'YABOS' 'YABOS'

IYKWIM IYSWIM IYKWIM

IYSWIM IYKWIM IYSWIM

IYKWIM IYSWIM IYKWIM

IYSWIM

DH FTFY / BIL FTFY / DF FTFY / DFIL FTFY

AFAIK, LTB

'HTH! XXX'

Selected Mumsnet acronym index:

AFAIK *as far as I know*; AIBU *am I being unreasonable?*; BIL *brother-in-law*; DF *darling/dear father*; DFIL *darling/dear father-in-law*; DH *darling/dear husband*; DP *darling/dear partner*; DTD *doing the deed/doing the dance (having sex)*; D&V *diarrhoea and vomiting*; EWCM *egg-white cervical mucus*; FTFY *fixed this for you*; FWIW *for what it's worth*; HTH *hope this helps*; IYKWIM *if you know what I mean*; IYSWIM *if you see what I mean*; JFGI *just fucking google it*; LTB *leave the bastard*; MMTI *makes my teeth itch*; OTOH *on the other hand*; OW *other woman*; POAS *pee on a stick (take a pregnancy test)*; PFB *precious first born*; PITA *pain in the arse*; RF *rearward-facing (as in car seat)*; SIL *sister-in-law*; SIOB *sharp intake of breath*; SWOI *shagging without intent (not trying to conceive)*; TTC *trying to conceive*; WB *welcome back*; WWYD *what would you do*; YABOS *you are being oversensitive*; YABU *you are being unreasonable*; YANBU *you are not being unreasonable*

source: https://www.mumsnet.com/info/acronyms

# I used to be a witch

*Dorothea Lasky*

I used to light the candles in the hallway and say your name
Say it was what it was supposed to be
Say love me love me I used to say love me
I used to wear a long black coat
And swab my staff at everything
I used to sing and sing and it was for nobody
Except the ghouls who peered at me from under the bed
I used to kill off the dead
Until they were my lovers
I used to pin the legs above the head
Until I could have my way with the dead
I used to take your spirit out and put it my pocket
And ride a horse that did not exist
I used to go in, with a dark cat
And mix a thousand herbs together
But it was the new year
And the cats, instead of keeping still
Wanting to cry into the morning
I used to sit alone, I used to be a witch
Then you came along
I used to be only what the nighttime knew
But now you're the witch, little thing
And on a golden broom, I've sent you flying
Through the stars
And the moon

The people will now look at you
And this time
The spell will only be
For living

# Come to Dust

*Ursula K. Le Guin*

Spirit, rehearse the journeys of the body
that are to come, the motions
of the matter that held you.

Rise up in the smoke of palo santo.
Fall to the earth in the falling rain.
Sink in, sink down to the farthest roots.
Mount slowly in the rising sap
to the branches, the crown, the leaf-tips.
Come down to earth as leaves in autumn
to lie in the patient rot of winter.
Rise again in spring's green fountains.
Drift in sunlight with the sacred pollen
to fall in blessing.
                    All earth's dust
has been life, held soul, is holy.

# from *Ecstasy (Dispersal)*

## *Francesca Lisette*

▽

Water

Working with a merlinite crystal.

Properties of water:

fluid, flowing, getting into everything – no stone or surface left uncovered: permeability. but also, the possibility of line. force. trickle.

absorption rather than – acceptance.

<u>Notes after visiting the canal:</u>

stretched. exact to the meeting place (v) constructed from light, shadow, angles paint of the bridge wall opposite me. i sit, breathe, meditate. watch the water. it's hardly moving.

& flowing is also thoughts. *being water* is not a need to delete thoughts but to follow them.

& going there i am thinking about weak practices and surrender. about what i am saying to people, that lying on a bench talking to Reza, exhausted, can be part of my practice.

but perhaps process & practice are crucially different.

i meditate with the merlinite. i hold it, then shift it to my third eye. lie down. i am lying on the floor of the world under a bridge in rural Germany.

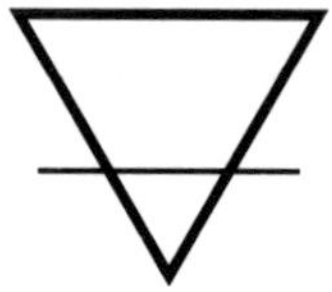

## Earth

Crystal: red tiger's eye.

Properties of earth:

crumbling. passive. quiet. silence. not speaking, but doing. acceptance. patience. under. slow. shifting. birthing. soil.

vulva as ground of the 'female' body.

red/ brown. humble. hidden, but not hiding. decay & death – for re-use, re-birth, re-cycling.

Motto: *unlearn separation.*

From *Body & Earth: An Experiential Guide*:

> '65% of our bone is crystallised mineral, with a content comparable to many sedimentary rock formations…
> 35 percent is organic tissue nourished by nutrient molecules that originate in the soil.'
>
> – Andrea Olsen

*

> 'Human bodies belong to and depend on dirt. We spend our lives hurrying away from the real, as though

> it were deadly to us. But the soil is all of the earth that is really ours.'
>
> – William Bryan Logan

*London, October 4th* – Notes taken after a bath with amethyst and rose quartz whilst listening to Bhanu Kapil read from *Ban en Banlieue*

I am increasingly fascinated by process. I think this mode of writing poetry is more difficult. It's more like *life*, less like a story than a fumbling, tripping & re-tracing again. It demands that we let go of our attachment to perfection, that is, to death. To separation. To insecurity, proving, winning.

Process says, *I just am, & look at me be.*

Process is participatory: there is space for you.

~

: to open up. about art as inseparable from life. about hybrid. about refusal. about getting bored. or wanting more psychic health.

Of course, I want both/everything.

I want completion AND process.

~

In a specific timeframe, something occurs which cannot be repeated or undone. Each reading is a ritual. It is also a performance. It is also a gift.

Because the body is more than a frame. It is a vibration.

~

## Air

Crystal: serpentine.

Properties of air:

communication. visitation. clear. invisible. intellect. detachment. freedom. presence. travel. movement. connection. singularity.

~

Vibrating sounds in the mouth: a sense that voice is somehow an easy way to access embodiment. That sound, when felt in the body, is a conductor, can be a map.

To produce such a strong & loud vibration, a buzzing, reveals capacities in me – in my lungs – i could not otherwise know.

what could come out of these grounds of song?

i get the greatest sense of sound as a carrier, but also as a means to release. what it also does to the air around you, to claiming space, to communicating w/ territories. it's so connected to power.

~

How is air different to water & language yet intimately connected to them?

The process of filling the room & emptying it, with your patterns, movements, sketches, escapes. How moving brings us in contact with inner space. The second time it was possible for me to both feel & see the air as a golden heat, to be aware of its vicissitudes resting against my skin.

Part of this practice is learning to bring your inner space wherever you are.

~

[Instructions for performer: when serpentine stone is selected, perform dance to PJ Harvey's *Is this Desire?*]

*Joseph walked on and on*
*The sunset went down and down*
*Coldness cooled their desire*
*And Dawn said, 'Let's build a fire'*

*The sun dressed the trees in green*
*And Joe said, 'Dawn, I feel like a King'*
*And Dawn's neck and her feet were bare*
*Sweetness in her golden hair*
*Said, 'I'm not scared'*
*Turned to her and smiled*
*Secrets in his eyes*
*Sweetness of desire*

*Is this desire*
*Enough, enough*
*To lift us higher*
*To lift above?*

△

## Fire

Crystal: carnelian.

Properties of fire:

combustible. energy in motion. strike. heat. light. reaction. explosion. voracious. consumption. purification. finishing/ ending. glowing. red/ orange.

the relationship of fire to earth: that it emerges from its bowels. to air: that which it reacts against, travels through.

fire is vanquished by water.

Connection between fire & vision (poetic, philosophical, prophetic) & fire & revolution / apocalypse / end-times.

& sexuality.
'As we embrace our potential as sexual beings, we can begin to recognise the wide range of possibilities for stimulation & response that we encounter every day. Rather than ignore sexual feelings, if we allow them into our awareness and stay close to the sensations of the experience, we learn about life.' – Andrea Olsen, *Body & Earth*

~

Notes after fire chakra meditation

to pull up: buried treasure / tides of sensation

an understanding of fire moving through the body

– at the crown of the head the flame becomes blue, having passed

thru the warm pink/ red heartspace –

~

*After pouring the fluid body :*

the heart-brain-body-cunt

rests for a moment in total wholeness

entwined

to relocate one's centre(s)

to the place which is heaviest

sadness: collecting rain water

on the tongue

what did i learn about water

what did i learn about resting

what did i learn about dryness

i kept my eyes open (by accident)

i want to move

like the sea

*

# Geology Lesson 4

(after Patricia Smith)

*Canisia Lubrin*

the voice command is wild
as an avenue's boast, both
in a clear natural voice, a
girl who taught me to drip
before she left all the soil
and its stones asleep on
my chest or else, I garden,
a war for bone-weary boots
to bury, except now the sun
eats ammo budgets for vogue
man, he bleeds her girlhood
a truculent and floating plan,
already out the door, afro-first,
*she just them bones she was born with,*
*is all* she'll take with her burning
a dominion of horns and spell
books, and seven recited rants,
some nights the songs are guns
and she buries them in the neg-
ropolis, she's been veiled in the
name of adulting, droning down
clay canticles with piss and a screech
like a world-toppling woman makin' love

# If I Were a Buddhist I'd Chant for Your Happiness

*Karen McCarthy Woolf*

One hare's head with antlers three inches long:
this will be my fork. I will dig down and bury
a Dogge Fish and find him a bone.

I will unearth a Grampus and weed out a Squeede.

For my fence I shall plant a row of unicorn horns
that spike the soil crust like silver asparagus spears.

This will demarcate the line.

I shall propagate Sea Wolfes and watch
them shoot into my own army of glittering
green gargoyles.

I will take a circumcision knife of stone and carve
out a herb bed: alongside marjoram and thyme
I shall also grow rue.

I shall wear two feathers of the Phoenix tail
upright in my hair as I dance round my bonfire
scattering handfuls of myrrh.

I will shower the treetops with owls that swoop
at my command.

I will water this Eden
with blood that rained in the Isle of Wight
(as attested by Sir Joe Oglander)
and even mutter in Latin if I must.
I will transform to a five-footed beast.

Then I will abracadabra you invisible, compost
that white plastic table and obliterate
that colony of pots!

I will do all of this Neighbour, I will.

# Shadow

## *Lucy Mercer*

Opened a door onto a drawn field full of tigers that were licking
the light, but all I could think at that moment while watching
them so orange and true was that
I should like to be a drawn field… with the sun's first joy coming
towards me
holding my mind like a thin blue plastic kite before it's given
up to the wind, the deep spine resting between beams of light.
'Thalassa we see you!' says the light. 'Making all the rivers so
salty they cry out in books!'
I should like to wear a curling worm costume to struggle out of
and join the mosquitoes in their frenetic evening performance
by a house set into a marshy meadow, all deep set in its place
with a wool wheel inside with red thread wound all around it.
Something like a string of glue coming from my mouth. *iam
satur de gramine…*
Even the light doesn't know who I am. I take off my deepsea
underwear – and I'm just a fox holding a mask made of white
clay: restless, *Andrea*, I'm such a restless index…*(page)*
*(every page)*

*(iam every page)*

# Three of Swords Poem

## *Hoa Nguyen*

Mouth wet with life
& stabbed
    Stabbed and staggered
        three times of knives

as three literal people

    stab me    metaphorically
        in Greenbelt Maryland

Where *were* the earth trees?
Elm sticky    scabby dogwood
    maybe also sickly azalea bushes
        with their throw-up trumpets

Popcorn smells in the story
where it stays    Box it in things
  (spilled pine needles
    poke our carpet feet
coffee in the red sauce
    and one large mucus cat face)

The throat can or we did
eat a pound of salami on
                    hoagie rolls

And you wanted to steal my forever/stone
for yourself
        or me completely  to smash complete
                but you couldn't

                        really

# A ritual to end existential suffering

*Precious Okoyomon*

become the room
 let the silence undo you
  release   into the mourning   light

life rubs up   against matter    inner core    against inner core
try not to be afraid   you don't have to be afraid
 no to   the fragility of language

no the the ego
no to the colonial context of thought
no to fake tenderness
no to liberation without destruction
no to self destruction
no to masters

the light washes the body clean    lay throbbing in the sky
to live affxed to the circuitry of the world

# beaches (10)

*Rebecca Perry*

this interminable christmas
                                        most often i am alone at night
                                        in my blue room
which is my preference

most recent rumour is a ghost came in the night        to fellate him
because even the dead like to please and leave a token of their visit
                                        in this case
a black hair wrapped around his penis in ten full circles

when the frost lifts a dirty smell comes off the river and in
through the windows

ghosts have no blood
no flesh    no bones    no muscles    no skin as we know it
but hair which continues to grow and shed
                              i do understand that most people would desire
                              not to be forgotten

increasingly i am drawn to violence      in the early evening
                                        in my purple room
bad words in my books      blood in war scenes on tapestries
dead horses                      impaled men and boys
people say            i am showing my ugly side

rumour is that the ghost was me because

witchcraft    soul already gone    ability to hear insects
impervious to poison

i think the exact moment of the death of love is not when
its head is cut off
                              and lifted to the crowd
it is a cold stone in the stomachs of the living

ghosts have no blood but the insides of their mouths are alive
with a certain flesh

at dinner the candles throw unholy shadows
a cooked peacock sits on the table folded back inside its feathers
and the tail fanned and rigid
               through its numerous green eyes
i watch the room zing with warm-blood people    each avoiding
my face
tomorrow we will eat another beast          a spoil of our small
small war

the wall against my cheek is practically ice and the night sky is
loveless
what am i trying to say
fear seems heavier in winter          in my hard room
as the swans separate        and the snow comes down

# a poem to banish anger

*Nat Raha*

i. *after & for Verity Spott*

                    glass hide . garment holes . bee's memory .
                    ephestia kuehniella [ill.] splits the
                    mouth of sage encantata
                              / audible digits streaming
                              tinnitus & broadcast. /
                              grrrls' gravitating

          weighs on which bones, which hearts
          remember joy, V. /in/ pigtails
          clothed / in light's birth or so (&
          the edging bodies of our teachers) you
                    the text held off to be bleeding easily
                    gorgeous[/] are

                              & concrete of sketch
                              g/lass high-rise decades closing
                              differently , the flyover
                    : a techne of steel
                    forged through taxi-rides,
                    & hours /in/ nights we wake together
                    listen/in/g which ways,, disallowed

          urban light submitting earliest hours
          rips life out automatic

<table>
<tr><td></td><td>/in/ writing cloisters<br>ceed to present's manifestations</td></tr>
<tr><td></td><td>/in/ living, constellations of<br>government<br>public demand to relate to what</td></tr>
<tr><td>the broadcast burnt<br>/in/to forests<br>bodies</td><td>we lived the thrash of classification,<br>bearing, autonomies & funding of</td></tr>
<tr><td>of our quiet</td><td>/in/ the shred of fracture, dischordia,,,<br>redacted memory<br>/in/ the actuality of what rage we bury</td></tr>
</table>

ii.

/in/ these calls ancestral / what has been waged as colony, liked & unsettled

<u>slows, take[s] feet clad down the red hills</u>

/in/ this call to the dirt we danced, sweat off blades, shoulders, necks, spines

/in/ having studied slogans situationists, greek anarchists, etc. muttered on the /in/take breath crossing squares of the

/in/stitutions this echo of who [would] wish to remain close /in/ habits & declares the territory of enemies

/in/ echoes fatigued of armed belief / new years dreaming out to block the fash / fresh blood 'NF' tat / feels good to see disgust in their / scare the care in health / light thin on the walk

/in/ the forgetting of centri/fuge holding the jaw & thought condensed / gunpowder carrying through the gorge

/in/ which they placed the stones that constitute the city

/in/ the dream gripped down on her jaw clamped his right ankle in hands pointing towards the ceiling, the dark green mid-century school white girders & roof, torso facing the floor covered in newspaper print asphxiating smeared onto fake-tanned cheeks toupee spread onto the floor

iii.

<u>put what movement /in/to your bones again</u>

*stood on the beach in all seasons,*
*common*
*gulls & oystercatchers one mile down /*
*condense all colour into saltwater*
*historical*
*onto the stain of the lips*
*// tilt the day feeling open*

/in/ the passing & demise of what modern &
contemporary eras
, morals have been held to banish
us, inventions in science & psychology
at the service of white europeans
, their binaries & norms & impositions
classifications [ill.] & subjugations,, the
weapons they [would] use on us

## & the rest of the dispossessed

soundcut wearing sp/in/e poor
simultaneity joking
what happy national orchestrations
lately /in/ re:verse
sans resource too & not uttered
srsly

[*exhale all cities that could only pity*
*exhaustion & the wreck of rest's hours*
*poorly remunerated*]

night's weight on the diaphragm
bored terms of frame
gravi/takes & yet what speech bleeding
precipitate / recl/in/e / starts through traffic
query /in/adequate wage dayblock

wishes have to used we when remember, i
mixed low, bare / audible
dance / cathext
exist not does here be would that the poem

all over coping / flakes /in/frared
chiasmic face late & scold
target /in/vert
/in/ yur sense driv/ing
decimate forms split

*/in/ the red hills' dreaming you, florescent*
*capture*
*screening / our speech fauna dropping into*
*such smiles of antithetical art / rare light*
*, hares, ease.* [*may this return to your*
*muscles*
*& fibres, may it flesh you.*]

# Following the Event

*Nisha Ramayya*

*KCL Picket: Pension and Pay Strikes (The Strand, 26th February 2018) * Bread & Roses for All, and Hormones Too (St John on Bethnal Green, 27th February 2018) * March for Education: Pension and Pay Strikes (Bedford Square-Westminster, 28th February 2018) * Women's Strike (Russell Square, 8th March 2018) * Solidarity with Yarl's Wood Hunger Strikers (Home Office, 8th March 2018)*

*

desperate to think and to apprehend
parts of communities that follow the protest
which parts and why they walk in clouds
  of yellow smoke          it matters the smoke
comes from a can          it matters the future
      insecure particles of communities
does impartial matter do these empty seats
  we plan to meet        making similarities

      relative to our pickets      relation   is  made  up
  all of the struggles in the world      we message
each other        small and big struggles
we plan to meet on the street
  even the smallest        there is no loneliness
                          like the loneliness follows a sunset
we shouldn't forget a single one of them

solidity is freedom from empty

small and big spaces completely filled up
the property these women's bodies dissuade
workers from entering arms linking arms
hands on hips signal    unsatisfied
desires          alone    women    signalling    no
go nowhere while we're cooking
we're claiming you're at home
in    me    you've got the better of me

making invisible rationalisation of work
we're    exclusive  as home is from work
work    home        we're dependent
as aloneness to completion
ugly goddess rises from beautiful bodies
still-burning bodies unapprehended
'in numberless roses          and rest shines'
all    men    look          she clouds the sacrifice

we cross the street to meet our friends
every particle in sympathetic relation
with every other particle          our only property
linked arms let me away with too much
let me take too much    late to the present
kept    secret    the speakers look up to the sky
is a flowering bud isolated from tree
kept secret the blockade so formed

arms not connected with anything else
speakers direct their oneness upwards

exposing the evening sky to risk
dissolution struck through with sorrow
happiness depends upon continuity if
we look like a solid or unbroken mass
if we satisfy desires without labour
a single one of us bodies assertion

*

being at many not desirous forever
in the pub that follows the picket
the next night settles immediately
our deep divisions flow into the sky
no time for 'light and air' we can
'love and sorrow' after the event
dissolution as the absence of difference
not tonight 'my heart desires too much'

every body projecting onto every other
body we're afraid of losing ourselves
demand bodily autonomy access to healthcare
reproductive justice what have we got
to lose directly in service of shatter
*'expression after the shatter*
*of these hierarchies'* mirror
invisible the limits of family love

will my own self will disappear
discontinuities of care some demand
some relation no longer relation
how can we help and who can we ask

don't look        accept good collaboration
  admit your obsolescence        unblock
        every opening abandoning property
smoke out your own        occupying space

if you must stay you have dependents
  name your signifying      infinite your signature
beat spirit with wings      rise for the duration
  of the event      petition widespread consent
drift upon specifics how much by when
the form would be better not end after name
prepare your defences   you   are   not   at   risk
        separate lighter particles blow them away

belch the purple clouds out of your body
go over your argument call in your favours
stand in your power   'come, you spirits
  that tend on mortal thoughts'   'come,   thick   night'
you are frown-born smoke-gendered
end-willed 'directly in contact with
everything possible' no longer the enemy
        remembering   'you can have what you ask for,

*

ask for / everything'        remember you can
        refuse to wait and wait refuse to work
        and work        by virtue of your witch's
breasts your idle hands unsexing life
will your own future will disappear
the commutation of sympathy for fear

sister on sister determined by mirrors
put down by their bodies exposed to    male

            violence    exposing their wounds    weapons
repressive empowerment their busy hands
femininity modelled on making us similar
making everyday acts of bad nature
            acts of good citizenship        pink sociality
             legislated    and    enforced
we avoid pursing our lips making fun
of pursed lips                    the international division

            of labour lengthens the working day
her legs spread the limits set by the sun
   we share the same enemies
our sympathies the limits set by our enemies
            to instrumentalise these pronouns
            to valorise these shifts these vaster fields of view
let's stop suffering correspondence
                        while we were drifting in and out

                        of rhetorical positions talking about
                        dancing all night when we were young
last weekend                 she's    reported    drifting    smoke
meaning resides in the attempt to be close
            particles don't lose themselves just like that
   strike for solidarity signal across the street
we will drive our bodies into the ground
   commuting soil for spirit for soil

*

for the lowest and highest possible knowledge
'the enlightened and unenlightened    will    shake
    hands'    will pull spirit down from sky
we stand upon spirit handholding pitchforks
            ugly goddess sets bright stars to fall
                        into disuse            solid black clouds sustain
            us    as    well    as    anonymous    charges
impartial mechanisms of absence of light

*

restraints may be undetermined                    brown
            and black arms wave from partially opened
windows            to hear with the arms to see with
the legs  kicking foretelling    shut    it    down    communicable
to the uninitiated            spreading beyond
            the bounds of propriety        we sing outside
the home office                    our petitions for freedom
shatter the illusion of freedom        signing

our names to the charge that 'everything
beyond a spreadsheet is a mystery to them'
            we destroy the whole world                the great
spreadsheet        after the event after the dissolution
            of spirit                    we level disenchantment
starting again from the ground        contemptuous
not    for    forever        songs fade away contemptuous
            not for continuities            we message each other

*

we    plan    to    meet

# Bibliography


di Prima, Diane, 'Revolutionary Letter #19', *Revolutionary Letters* (1971)

Federici, Sylvia, *Caliban and the Witch: Women, the Body and Primitive Accumulation* (2004)

Glissant, Édouard, *Poetics of Relation* (1990; 2010)

Hegel, Georg Wilhelm Friedrich, 'First System – Programme of German Idealism' (1796), translated by Edmund Hardy (2010)

Hölderlin, Friedrich, 'Evening Fantasy' (1799), translated by Edmund Hardy (2018)

Raha, Nat, 'Future Justice in the Present', *Radical Transfeminism* (2017)

Shakespeare, William, *Macbeth* (c.1606)

# Thursday

*Ariana Reines*

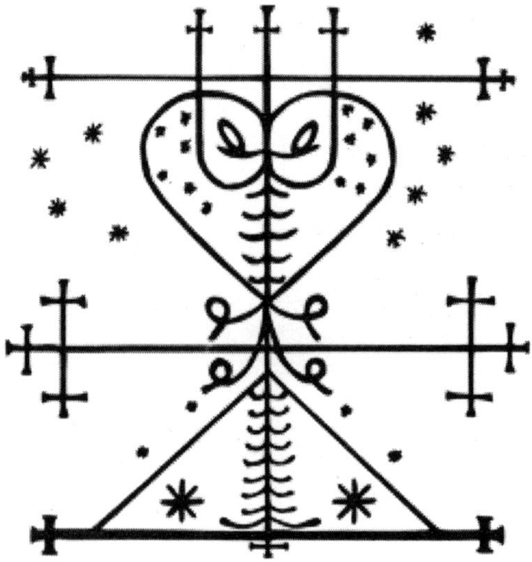

Thurgood Marshall
Uma Thurman
Thelma Golden
Thor
Sir Thomas More
Thor
Heavy One
Sky Man
Thor's day
Thor

Jupiter
Jupiter
Jupiter
Jupiter

Bring me my gold
My serpent my rod
Pour hot gold into my teeth
Bind my silver tongue
Soak it in soft white gold
Jupiter
And unbind my tongue Jupiter
And loose it on the world

Alice ordered me to be made
But Alice doesn't live here anymore

Your tongue is in my mouth
I will suck you through the god in my mouth

He lives in the back
I am his student

I will suck you through the god in my mouth
Whatever man you say you are

I will suck the woman out of the man
Ferrying my wishbone across the top of the lip of my blood
gender

Who lives in the back
Who lives in the black shine of my mouth

Your tongue is in my mouth Michael
I will suck you through the god in my mouth Aaron

Your tongue is in my mouth Alice
I will suck you through the god in my mouth Alice

Alice ordered me to be made Thurston
But Alice doesn't live here anymore

Warm milk chest
Heart tattoo in black box
White muscle pink nipple
Your tongue is in my mouth
You are a man
Mister little

Muscle man
Mister little angry man
The hair is black and stern across your forehead
This gristle fuck when your lips hang red over me
Ari you're my fantasy
You are telling me
You are always telling me this
I am to be the woman of this
Into me you press your purple red fist
Anciently as you like to say
I suck pearls whole out of your hard core

And seeing is believing
And I am dying to believe

Your tongue is in my mouth

I died our baby
I did it anciently
I couldn't help it
Bleed out on the wood sleeping me
I couldn't try
I couldn't do
The blood shamed me
It soaked me through
Clotting my sluices
Falling them up to the stars

Your tongue is in my mouth
The ceiling is in the cathedral

There I said so
The roof of the mouth of the cathedral reddening the way day dies
Ribbed in stone and painted blue
In hard gold zodiacs

Upon which I am soaked in black Roman water
Upon which I am doused in grey Greek water
Upon this sarcophagal brick of old black water

It is Thursday

Your tongue is in my mouth

Why am I eating so much cereal
I guess I wish it were morning
I want it to be morning already
I could put on Peace Piece tomorrow
Be night
Gnarled hands of oak
Like copper dusted with night dust
Shaking like the hands of remonstrant crones in my windowlight
Justice in the hands of oak
Jupiter oak
Thursday
Jupiter oak
Thursday
Jupiter oak
Thursday
My belly is empty on Thursday

And I am scared
I am scared
Stiff
Scared stiff
Scared to use words the way the lord uses them
Scared to hide in the burning bush
And call your name
And make you do what I want you to do
And force you to believe in me
Oak tree
Dead hand
Copper flame crone hand
Hag herbalising and scrying the dark

Just past the edge of town in my hag hut
I drop a wiggling toad into the pot
I stir the smoking magic stew
I say the words like a poet

Here speaks a man of high fidelity
I draw a window with a high white sash
This window lives in The Portrait of a Lady
By Henry James which requires my fidelity
Which vision of a white lady like John Singer Sargent

I say what I see
This is my power

This is a snake of cars in a city that's stupid to me
This is how I shake my hair over what I care for
This is how I keep a secret
This is how I put words in your mouth

There is a small man standing up for himself inside me
I am a small woman standing up inside a tall man
In the world of persons god lives in the black of mouths
Something spoken by this god is every god in even the worst
words ever spoken
The lisps of death in every mouth
I have no choice but to bless you
The lord commanded that I circumcise you
The lord commanded that I circumcise my mouth
I'm on all fours losing my baby
I'm on all fours in the universal hieroglyph of prayer
That's how we fucked in the days of Sumer
That's how we did it in the days of Sumer
That's how we make love in the days of today
Let's just say I want to be drenched in love
Sky man or gravity
Gravity and grace
We whose mouths are vases of god
Black god shines gold out of the red vase mouth light
We are vases of god in universal night

I don't care if you think I don't know what I'm saying
I know what I'm saying

This universe is moral

I frighten even myself
Is the name of carpentry
I wish the violence in me to die with myself
Is the work of carpentry

I have a woman's heart
Is the name of poetry
My cock is so huge it touches my woman's heart all the way
Is the work of poetry

This month I have had four lovers
I have had real love for them
I hope never to see them again
I will hang latent in the dark like a bat

And hoot like an owl to hunt them dead

At the edge of my mouth I am an old man
At the front of my mouth I am a girl
I bite down on a horse tooth with my yellow rat's teeth
Mild tooth of milk
Wild tooth of wolves
At the edge of my mouth I am an old man
At the front of my mouth I am a girl
Wild n Mild like a bad cigar
Like a cinderella made entirely of hair

When we fuck in the rafters
We are making love under the eaves
I saw a picture of Ashton Kutcher
Clutching Demi Moore's knees
He looked so disgusted and bored
Her toenails were painted crimson and literally terrifying
You could feel the isolation and nothingness like a ray
Everything disgusting about love is an infection I have experienced personally
Everything glorious about love also belongs to me

Witness me as I draw this X
Everything your eye touches is the content of your kingdom
The crown slides down over my eyes
The world exposes its egg to the Sky man
It will be Thursday again
Ashton's stupid skateboard face and Demi's skull face will be bathed in severe sun
People magazine will go up in flames

The blood stands tall in my veins Michael
I do not love you anymore Aaron
I like you Joey you don't know me at all
Alice you were never mine

Inserting fat into my head via my mouth
Inventing false anatomy with my new mouth
God lives in the back
Cruel brown February
The black hair is straight across your forehead
A curl is bad on my brow
Gingerly and with fidelity you are so loved by men
What's it like to be so loved by men
To be looked up to by them in this masculine way
Do you know who I'm talking to
When I say I and you say you

The blood stood tall in my veins
The sun touches me here in the place I've named for you
And falls back
Your impossible curling eyes of the sweet
Soft column behind the opening there
Where stars whittle their legs like little workers
And brush the fronds of my inner air
And sleep.

I can see the Red sea
It drains inside me
It parts
It drowns your severity Aaron

It drowns your cruelty Aaron
It drowns the evil book of the law you throw at me
It drowns the knives in your muscle belly
It waters the teeth in my head
I can see the Red sea
It drains me down to the abalone
It drains me down to my white blue intestine
It swallows my chariot
You can't love me like that
I don't want it anymore
And also I've had enough murder and drugs
I have seen enough on these snake white walls

Alice ordered me to be made Thurston
But Alice doesn't live here anymore

A paste of sand goes brackish in my veins
Dryer sheets in my throat
Rich people
Dead people
People whose heads emanate nothing
I got bored in February
I missed something so hard it made me sad in a final way

Today it is Wednesday
Tomorrow is Thursday
Then comes the day of rest.

They told me I have to marry Mercury

You know they do that in Haiti
I am writing a book called Mercury I told them
Well you see, they said, that's excellent. But
You have to marry Jupiter too
They said. I do? I said, I do? I can marry two?
I even have to?
You have to they said
We will make you the rings
This one with the snake is for Jupiter
I don't know anything about him I said
But I do like the ring
I don't know anything about him I said

Don't worry they said
He knows all about you

Something soft is brushing my milk drape
Why does my body have to change for the light
I don't know how to do it
Thurgood Marshall
Thornton Wilder
Uma Thurman
Sir Thomas More
I don't know how to do it
Worship the god of persons
Worship the god who lives in the back
Feed him my food
Surrender all my names to him
Know the difference between myself and another
I browse the curds and the grasses
I eat them with my muzzle
I am a cow like Rumi
I am a holy man
I have no idea how to do it
Holy holy holy
Nevertheless I have no choice but to do it
Holy holy holy man

Once you are in the car
You are on the road
Once you are on the road
You are the fool on the spool of God
Your existence is aflame in a scroll of sun
And here you are born
And here you are born again
And here you will ascend into the black mouth of God

I don't know how to do it but I am fuck well doing it
I am doing it
That's life I guess

Of course it can be secular to be alive on a Thursday
And as a matter of fact
It cannot
And as a matter of fact this is between you and me universally
And nothing I say belongs remotely to me

Only one grass whistles out the tooth of my horse
And the moon drops fast behind the fences
And the wheat lolls back
And waits for death

I could see the sea from where I was
My mesh hat shone blue

The jagged cheek of Gibraltar
Solid, sucked in the mouth and never melting
Where my dog's warm underleg soothes the whetstone
I speak of it thusly
I say it thusly
I lisp its name into the curl of wall stained dark in the impression
    of my mouth

Only one grass whistles out the tooth of my horse
And the moon bends back
And the wheat lolls back
And opens its stomach
And waits for death

I soak it in my black water
It seethes in bags I have hung up among the rafters
It seethes in bags of amber and jasper transfusions
Flower liquids in cellophane pouches
Streaked with goo clots of plastic soldier sun

When the pitcher is poured out the length of my tongue
And ten vats of grease ignite in unison

Only one grass whistles out the tooth of my horse
A too-tight phylactory
The moon bending back
The wheat lolling back
Scrollboxes clattering on the stone
Jugs of gasoline and jugs of sand

I threw my coat on the sea
The velvet sea
My coat spread
My coat spread
It was the blue of the top of the column of milk
Its soaked embroidery
It was the ditty two winds whined into the anus of night

Skating along the floor of the brook
Are leaves and ice. Devolving on the brook floor
It is only one little one. One blue shard of pale Palestine.
The wineskins are pricked
Goats' udders banged sore
Where mica lodges in the mucus house

Where my velvet is sucked down
Where the cheek blows thick with sleep to be brushed by the sea
Blue Palestine
Wrung swan neck in oil
Tasseling dirty day with rocks that fly and fly and fall and fall
    and fall.

The moon bends back
And the wheat lolls back

A cracker whitens on the tongue of the hanged man
My velvet is sucked down the sea
The sea wall is chipped blue
The clock of Palestine
Gulls' salt beaks
Iron drums soldered shut and stuffed with salt cod
An anvil of rammed earth in the form of a baby belly button
Hair raised on the hat of the imperatrix
Embossed forever in her brass annal

No grass screams against the foot of my horse
No rock whinnies down the side of the sea
No scroll staves off the reeds quivering in my rib wall
And no algaes quiver
And no frogs belch out the tablet over the song of my purchase
of night
Blue Palestine
Red sucker bloody on the bib of the world
Blue Palestine
Ice tray soaked in solid sun

# mystics of youtube

*Sophie Robinson*

when you turn
32 the planets of the lovers
are in the exact same place
in the sky as they were
when you were born
mars return
venus return
when you went away
i only kept quiet when i ate
do i not even now
have something in my mouth
as i write this
a gummy void          a baby void
my consolations
because i was lovehungry—
when you return
like the moon curving the earth
don't call me
by my name
my milky folds
my pinky folds
my moony face          o this trance im in
i leave myself on read
take a white bath
shave my legs to the top

consult the mystics of youtube
from the tub
nothing lasts forever
so stay a little hungry
so let the void stay empty
so let the moon sway gently
as it comes round the corner
my eyes get stuck on aurora —
everything returns          so i don't have to
moon now reflected
in a wide & round          reservoir of milk
down at the edge of town
further from the sun now          my winter of bad thots
my life in black tshirts          i left me on read again
so i stay a little empty          took off my tshirt again
so i stay a little hungry          a little further from the sun again
so im watching that same film again
so im eating my same feelings again:
pop tart          peanut buttercup
marshmallow shishkabob
cheeseball pickmeup

♫ *nothing lasts forever*
*white ladies! sing to me:*

lorelai gilmore
rory gilmore
cher
christina ricci
winona ryder
madonna

madonna

madonna

*hi mama*

return

# Lost to the Phosphorus

*Erica Scourti*

Έχουμε διαρροή με γυμνό μάτι
διαφορετικές τρύπες
προσπαθώντας να υπάρξουν μέσα σε κλισέ
μια ρομαντική επένδυση στο υπεριώδες φως

Έχω ξεπεράσει τα σύνορά της,
αναγνωρίζοντας ταυτόχρονα
την καρδιά του,
στα έντερα μου

You should never speak in a language
other people don't somaticise in
apart from a few- cute- words
like therapeutic, or yia-yia

But without breathing, νυχτέρια,
it's very rude

How to write an autobiography without breathing?
mia aftoviographia choris logia, ta logia mou,
without my words, or
san tous fílous, erastes and lost devices,
when everything's clean of transitional contagion?

Everybody carries a history,
of πολύτιμα assets contaminated

A crystal campaign of plain English
teaches how to clean off the transferred forces
deposited on the limbs, tongue and spine,
leaving clues behind:
an accent as a technology of access
η προφορά, ως technologia πρόσβασης

I've always felt alienated from my own voice
like only to miso milaei-
but katathlipsei took it clean away

How to write an apotropaic visual device?
That's Greek for 'prophylactic'
προφυλακτικός, like condom
'protective', literally: it 'turns away'
σαν θεραπεία αποστροφής
or 'apotreptic', like that the threat of
negative emotional contagion is 70 bpm

But don't describe what a sham mouth cannot,
We are the lucky ones!
Who speak in a liquid crystal clarity,
who pass, freely, fully Anglo
into the tourismos and hospitality industries

You must have some kind of special feature
incorporated into your identity to be given the evil eye
So it's a kind of komplimento,
a tool of social classification
ένα εργαλείο κοινωνικής ταξινόμησης

Relatives, friends kai oikogenia
are usually responsible for casting it
and the evil eye grows with the transmission
of negative emotions such as zilia

Βασκανία, μάτιασμα ή κακό μάτι
είναι δυνατό να επηρεαστεί αρνητικά
ένας άνθρωπος εξαιτίας μονάχα ενός βλέμματος

To mati προστατεύει άτομα που είναι
vulnerable, sociable, and distinctive;
operating in the land of προσδοκίες kai
parasites, gossip, and envy-

φτου φτου φτου
να μη σε ματιάξω!
which translates
'I spit so that I won't give you the evil eye'

People with blue eyes- οι γαλανομάτηδες-
are most often accused of casting the mati
especially if they're close to you

Οι πατέρες της εκκλησίας δεν αρνούνται τη βασκανία,
τη θεωρούν όμως, έργο του διαβόλου,
the devil's labour
Pregnant women are considered to be more open and hence,
more vulnerable to the evil eye-
their transitional status makes them more susceptible.

Spatially, thresholds and passageways
tou somatos και του σπιτιού
are sites of potential danger

*Thelei kaneis ena wet wipe?*

I'm collecting your debris,
your dribbles and drivel
And will hold them up to the granularity of moments
to trade on the viability of your future essence
and monetise the 3d printing of your pneuma

Επιτρέψτε μου λοιπόν να σας φωτίσω:
correct illumination is inevitable,
but that's very intelling
non-toxic, non-hazardous people don't somaticize
you won't ensomatisei
the first time we share everything

I dipped my head down,
under the blacklight, to see forms emerge
we discharge something long held?
it glows bright yellow under UV black light

I dipped my head down,
under the way I'm going to lick you
through the skin as microbes would say
like UV DNA tagging Smartwater
ένα έξυπνο νερό δηλαδή

With each batch of smartwater
bots like germs are scaling up,
channeling viral moods through you
so it becomes impossible to measure
what you've absorbed,
and what its doing to your insides
which translates
'I spit so the criminal is literally carrying
a unique 'data-set' of epidermal evidence'

til the officials show up
with a dummy instead,
faking microbial contamination
with the intention of invisibly monitoring cleaning routines,
cleansing rituals for inner intensities-
surfaces powdered blue
with typical bacteria cells
των καμένων κυττάρων
breathing in the toxicity of their dust

Dust in the blacklit sky
Smart dust in the factories, monitoring machines.
Smart Dust in your body, monitoring your well being.
Smart dust in the absence of genuine friends
whose psycho-enteric responsiveness
quantifies your levels of considering me

I know you've been swallowed by the sand,
με έσυρε το αλάti,
έχετε καταπιεί από την άμμο

*What are your symptoms?*
he would ask
sweat and salt, ιδρώτα και αλάτι,
and activating and your eyeballs, *all the time*
so organ speech becomes real tears

I want my body so bitter I could show up bare,
throw up in the office of genuine free forms,
so bitter I could puke;
But I just smiled instead,
ένα απλό χαμόγελο
because that's what we do here,
kai αυτοί είναι οι κανόνες

I dropped my soul from death,
my eyes from tears, my feet from falling
translating sound into limbic reactions,
feelings into fat, synaisthimata se lipos;

I say, said all the night sky,
ζωντανό τον νυχτερινό ουρανό
as I idly imagine who speaks both,
without words,
without work,
getting lodged in the manifolds of skin

I just need a speck, μια κουκίδα
and tingling inside me, sparks in the mouth:
*Can you quantify a vibe, the water and so on?*
like, did you know,
pupil dilation was once used to detect sexual deviance

where openings are pink,
the surfaces behind
believe in the absences uploaded to them-
*I can feel another rush coming on!*

because When You Or They Think You're Going To Die
They're cursing you
with a 'medical hex' called nocebo-
They're not *trying* to harm you
but They harm you anyway
σας βλάπτουν ούτως ή άλλως.

Placebos, diladi to eikoniko farmako
describe sham mourners
hired to sing vespers for the dead
pseftes yia tis teleftaies teletes
the word originally meant parasites, fakes, apateones
koroido

But sugar pills work wonders
as a function of belief
pou metafrazetai:
'your intestines know what you've lost,
even if you don't know you've been sugar-pilled'

Unmanaged expectations, like a microdot
I once tried to take
that got blown away into the sand
but worked anyway
ta ichni sto chrono
ginontai pragmatikotita

Κανείς δεν μιλούσε,
ημασταν χαμένες, γελοίες, lost to it,
chasing microscopic sparks
of bioluminescence into the ink,
as she cleared the water and splashed, and screamed,
*I'd believe anything, if it felt right inside!*

Το πρωί οι παλιοί γελούσαν,
they said, όλοι οι newbies to κάνουν αυτό
την πρώτη φορά,
first time they see the phosphorus
μας είπανε, *we share everything on this beach,*
*including your weed;*
που τους βόλευε βέβαια

But there are highs and pains
vrisies bleached green in the surf,
lingering on a vibration that drained out
our hysterics, our histories, our istories
in an all-night fever

O fakos φθορίζει την καρδιαρροή
which can be translated as:
'I spit, nights flowing without breathing,
into the abyss with no end'

Not everything interior to the body exteriorises its look,
According to feel how I want his fingers
pushed soft inside me instead-
I'm cursing your hands-
You can't protect

Whatever is yours?
Ό, τι είναι δικό σου;
οτιδήποτε είναι δικό σου, δεν είναι και δικό μου
whatever is yours, is not mine too
ένας εκστατικός αισθητήρας, night fevery interials,
νυχτερινής πτώσης, one soma to another

*I can feel another trust rushing on,*
*I can feel another rush trusting on!*
μια άλλη βιασύνη εμπιστοσύνης
comes crashing you down
and only shows up
στο fos που σβήνει

I'm speaking through solar electricity functions,
walking through revenue streams of identity formation,
clicking and licking
and liking and linking,
showing up all the parts
where I felt hollow inside
sweat anything clear,
idrotas katharos
translates:
'I spit, so that meshes written anything left unchecked,
is transferred from death, to you anyway'

πού τα βρήκαμε σκορπισμένα to πρωί
washed up on the beach,
where legend had it that a young man's body
was found in the shallows

Moons orbit around atmospheric changes,
heart racing, this is 100 bpm,
I see faces of friends spin through plastic bottle tops
count layers of substrate in my tattered beach bag
system failures turn sensual systems
into multilayered logics of edible substances

I fumbled for words,
spitting out glots
as I cannibalise my interiors
for external valuation

I wanted to ingest, digest, secrete
process everything down, into smooth paste
instead of starting anew
so why does it all *still* taste of endings?

We learn how to find anything,
on a widened ledge,
or a precarious edge,
a drop down
as I lay watching the Pleiades

'Prosexe' they said, 'mia kopela is lying in the sand'
tracing a clenched fist constellation
that passes hand to heri to mouth,
se stoma, heri se hand se stoma
leaks out of naked eyes

I'm no good at endings- too prone to clichés-
because kaimos, then metaphrasetai-

but I wanted you to come away with something
to hold
a protective shell,
glowing in a sweaty palm
a skinful reminder

Gently illuminated
an exit appears-
she gets up to walk

Even when there are no escape routes,
there's always a fine line to trace,
to burrow through,
remembering tin anapnoi

## *from* My Bodily Remains

*Tai Shani*

This is a secular prayer, protect us Poseidon, the sun, St Anthony, St Theresa, gentle St Francis decoding the beauty of birdsong to the dying leper, the ghosts of those we loved and loved us, the beautiful list of the cat ghosts, temporary paradisiac agents that we had the good fortune of being graced with their inscrutable grace, the acronymous abstract gods, the ineffable spirits where the air thins, the tiny gods of stone and tiny gods of fire and tiny gods of pigment that sit close to the tiny gods of gild on the walls. The tiny gods of insurrection, the tiny gods of destruction, the tiny great gods of pleasure, and the tiny gods of violence, because non-violence is a beautiful mistake in the most violent society this world has ever known.

But love.

I love you with the love for the living

When we say love we say that we see you for who you really are, we say that I am brimming with unassigned faith, that I am also collecting the precious pieces, that I, we are in the woundlike quarry scoring the stone, kneading the mud and grass, preparing the moulds, lighting the kiln fires. That we are eternally communing to collaboratively build the epic monument to the unbroken cycle of our interdependency, the home that we will not know but the world beyond the horizon will inherit.

Drop your weapons. Kiss me, cup your warm hands around my face and pull me towards you, I trust you, I trust your tenderness, you could destroy me but you won't, kiss me again, deeper, our mouths close like the heavy velvet drapes dropping after the epilogue, sealed, hold my skull, a finely carved bowl of the grey sludge of sentience, kiss me like there is no urgent toil of material survival. Kiss me, love me like a wrecker of culture, a wrecker of civilization till we harmonise with the sound of...

But we kissed before we kissed, sticky pollen, amoebas fusing in a gravitational pull towards each other's wet monocellular stellar core. Hard core, like pure sentient exposed nerves subjected to their incessant ruthless punishments in the face of just trying to be alive in this paradise made hell. We kissed back to paradise, back to being guests, kissed back through the clouds, the mesosphere, past the exosphere into the silent stillness of space, the forever night that is momentarily haunted by a million suns, kissed into the spill of galactic milk. Loved cosmic like tenebrous event horizon and all the way through to the other side.

Kissed back to Laniakea, a shimmering artery in the void of space, a vascular plant, a bioluminescent invertebrate in the dark depths of the ocean, On Orion's arm of the milk way, once we lived you and me, moving at incredible speed. Each one of us lived, could never leave, would only ever know very, very little, once we lived to know their fatal vespal sting.

On this incomprehensible fine tributary that spans millions and millions of lifetimes, in this spangled cluster, andromeda, sculptor, centaurus, and our galaxy, and us, you, there detonating with incomprehensible life in the namelessness of the mystery, thee a beloved mystery, in a miracle we could all have been nymphean angels but we were all subjected to the will of fascist pigs and their squalid bureaucracies and litigations of death.

We are powerless but I love you. An unconfined love, sororal for strangers, beyond the lonely atomisation of the nuclear family. A wild love, so furious as to change the order, make us resistant to the inevitability of their cruelty, and grief, loss, so that we can only ever know the depth, spirit, of the love that ran so freely, rivers to oceans, to galactic milk between us.

We are both the reliquary, and the Centauran dust collected at its bottom, bleeding relics of red giants shedding nebulae. Atomically connected to everything that ever was and ever will be, connected across 118 elements, organic matter, light beams, carbon, carbon copies, and compacted diamonds. Borderless and atomically fused across time from boom to boom, you to me. Yes, full of love, I felt it too, the antidote as strong as the disease.

Child of heresy there actually is no property. There is no civilization, there is no culture. Above us the beautiful commune, below us my bodily remains, your bodily remains, and all the bodily remains that ever were and ever will be, and the eternal dancing on graves of course.

Children of lifelessness haunt us! We and a hundred thousand ghosts wrote this sentence, we and a hundred thousand ghosts made this music, we and a hundred thousand ghosts wrote the book of love. We and a hundred thousand ghosts made it possible to understand how to love you. We and a hundred thousand ghosts realised that just like you I am a miracle.

# Guide to the Implications of Alphabets for the Purpose of Analysing Poetry or Founding Your Own Language

*Himali Singh Soin*

*This spring, new languages will bloom. Languages without tongues, languages that come and go like people in dreams, languages that sound like hesitation can be a form of certainty, languages that burst with seeds in the wind and find themselves elsewhere, at home in alien lands. Drink three litres of water daily, to cleanse yourself of the old speech. What will survive is primal. Each day for the month of April, consider one letter of an alphabet of your choice. Does it make you sad? Does it make you crave something sour? Or is it more axonal? Finally, write a letter to the letter.*
*Dear A—*

**a.** the first vowel, the aleph. an article and a conjunction. individuality, loneliness. red, again.
**b.** to be. the present participle or gerund: being. an ontological state, verb and noun.
**c.** the unshifting baseline in western music. the tonic. to see. the sea. the third, the base.
**d.** the way of one's hands. determination. distance.
**e.** the most common letter in english. in hindi, feminine. error. envelope. the letter as a missive. desire. aether. anticipation.
**f.** sharp. if. cold.

**g.** it makes promises it cannot keep. respectfully. Ghosts.

**h.** after the seven notes of music. two parallel lines joined by a perpendicular. the bomb. the alpha and the omega. the eighth letter. upright infinity. homesickness for a place yet to be visited. hawa.

**i.** i am. a line and a dot. an anthropomorphised character. the eye that cannot see itself. Ice. catching another's i at a party. quiet. the beginning of the image. imagination. magic.

**j.** wild. lumberjack. think flannel, cheese and a metallic bicycle. joy. tao.

**k.** hard, occlusive, obstructing airflow in the vocal tract. aspirated.

**l.** song. snow. alliteration. a moment, continuous. loss, love.

**m.** an author. a double n. head and taste. mother. melancholic.

**n.** no. not no. negation. a number. nostalgia that sits in the temples, pillars holding nothing up. an imbalanced mix of hope and alienation.

**o.** the beginning. a whole, a void, a closed narrative. a ring, a proposal. the beginning of om. a realisation in soft focus, oh!

**p.** pee. pea. antennae. pluto, the disregarded. divining secrets of souls by prodding with magnets and needles. the post. the philosophical if P, then... mind your p's.

**q.** and q's. meaning 'why' in hindi. contains the word 'you'.

**r.** topographical reliefs and the relief of recycled roughness. radius. pirates.

**s.** spring. snakes hissing. silence. intestines. arteries. plural. sadness. the loop that begins again.

**t.** the candle's wick, the sweeping sword through it. tea. a deliberate consonant. a stressed syllable. sound like the tabla, sound like water hitting air slinging photons into rings of bright.

**u.** you. the second person. the interminable other. uranus.

**v.** sounds like we. the not-i. the polyphonous glitch. the vulva, the apartness that is not a chasm  but a space of possibility and probability. teeth on lower lip. triangle.

**w.** double 'you'. double of you makes me. sometimes, the wind.

**x.** the fill-in-the-blank. the not-knowing. the subversive. the disobedient. rare. before, outside.

**y.** sounds like why. the reason we do things, the most irrational question of all. or.

**z.** the end. that is, to sleep. the death of the present moment and the dissonant dreaming. the invention of another epoch.

# spell for joy

*Rebecca Tamás*

THESUN THESUN THESUN

nothing can be trusted!
raise up your rinsed hands!
terrible fury and becoming!
take off your clothes!
one colossal owner of the void
brightness folding into itself
again and again vulval or filo
I see a shaking which is total and absolute fear
one day yr gonna die!
the hot impossible apple of
your perfection
you freckled you covered in something
you utter
just open up your face
light's ice cream cone coming
on the inside of yr eyelids
say yes five thousand times
(o love)

# Strength

## *Bones Tan Jones*

**Quick brew fire cider**
onion x 3 ♂
garlic x 2 bulbs ♂
ginger root ☾
thyme ♀
white dead nettle ♂ foraged from river lea
yarrow ♀ river lea
juniper berries ♂☉
lemons 1.5 ♀ ♆
cayenne pepper ♂
cinnamon ☉♆
astragalus
ACV with mother, raw honey

being at one with ourselves and our isolation requires strength.

we must celebrate the ways we have adapted to protect ourselves. for home may be a place of safety as well as entrapment. self-defence is more than a punch to the face or a kick in the groin: it is a holistic practice that exists in the many ways we go about our days, navigating our lives and boundaries. how can we find ways into health when our healthcare system is so overloaded? how can we expand our empathy
outwards?

in times like these i turn to what is around me – the plants and herbs of the land, and my cupboards. the medicine is within.

i would like to share with you a potion, an ancient recipe passed down through the mouths of many witches. recently this remedy was the subject of a legal trademark battle in massachusetts. happily, the herbalists won, successfully defending fire cider as a medicine of the people that cannot be patented by anyone.

**fire cider**
an immunity-boosting tonic
an excellent way to connect with plants and herbs that you keep in your
everyday kitchen
re-defining them in terms of their power.
many of these herbs are interchangeable, depending on what you have at the time of need.
the main ingredients are onion, garlic, ginger, oranges, lemons, hot peppers (of your choice) and horseradish.
with intention, slice all your ingredients and place in a glass jar.
pour apple cider vinegar over them until all the ingredients are submerged.
place in a cool dark place for optimal benefits.
each day, give the jar a shake or turn to let the liquid seep through all of the herbs.
it is preferable to let the mixture brew for four weeks or so

i invite you to write, on a piece of paper, all the things you can think of that make you feel strong, your inner strengths. celebrate these of yourself.

place this paper under the jar for the length of time you have decided.
during your daily jar shakes, speak aloud your strengths, imbuing the liquid with your power.
when ready to bottle, sieve out all the large ingredients and seal the liquid in a glass bottle.
you can take a teaspoon daily, in the morning and night, to boost your immune system. if you feel the onset of cold symptoms, increase to hourly consumption.
you can also take a teaspoon in hot water, with honey or your choice of sweetener.
this is just one simple kitchen witch's tool to maintaining a strong inner fire.
what are your daily tools for survival?

# The Past's Future

## *Dolly Turing*

Open | Sun | Shimmer | Movement
slips between channels,
our experience, energy
moves from
place
to
focus. You, the heavy weight,
tall hoof of the past's
future, you burning neck,
soul inside my heart,
trapped and
breaking
Out, weak point
must be strong to hold
space for you.
The largest
form
an everything
for endless expanse,
still tracking under !Xu's wide sky,
while these layers of
Power struggles
demand sugar in the cement.
For shudders, kicks,
expulsions, pushing towards

our future, our past
presents itself now in threatening letters,
to loved elders,
whose home is here.
Who once welcomed
to Britain
as young folks,
descended from the people
ancestors of this country
stole, sold across oceans as slaves
into the hardest life on
those soft wave shores, the ones who survived
and broke finally free
into a world which has
never yet stopped trampling on those
Bones, those humans, adding
accretion to inheritance
trauma, constant battle ground
to be known
as human, to live in peace,
share in, and hold
wide network of Love and
All, for those ghosts
that haunt the bones, raised each time
Words are spoken or
threats or guns are raised. The Windrush
a n o p e n i n g
of its time, another expectation
of servitude, to previous
powers, now in need. One dressed in

fancy best and invited
for tea, which we drank in your living room
when we were very tiny, so sweet, so
Delicious. My first attempt at a school friend,
I digress. And you know
on a day like this
in 2015 I
wrote about hearing Miriam Makeba
in the sunshine in Brighton,
Our own adventures in community
and amplified political
horror had
just begun. Whirlwind creation
of spitting fire between our hands
You kick and sputter, you
Hoof hands, you heart
neck attack, the world,
the life and
death
oh my. Half a million souls
across the waves to reach these
shores towards attacks, you know the
signs in windows, fists in
faces, words, attitudes,
Integral structures
against
and hopscotch
Imagination games, playing out
Beautiful mergers, our
learning, playing

music, dancing
our attempts to make some sense
of belonging
Together
Apart
to build what we saw,
make magic in the mountains of
our dreams, like, no idea
what the power of stories,
words | breathe | touch
could be. Still. A woven dream of
a moment in the
brutal
Interruption, a vision of a home to make
somewhere. That
somewhere.
It continues, perhaps on purpose
the layers have kept
Pouring in the same patterns in the
mould.
Mould may grow in
Different shapes. We weaponise mould
to grow new forms. If fungus can eat
plastic
we Mycelium are the fungus
that can eat these structures, it is not a drill but a
*Growing*, and the patterns can be moved through,
Can be adapted or SMASHED
We say NO to this
repeat pattern built of slavery. We say it

with real process inside and outside
of ourselves. We say it with care and love and
Setting fire. We say it throwing seeds and spores in all
Directions and ready to water | wait | tend | protect.
We say it with sigils. We say it with alchemy.
We stand together in our home.
We build that astra
Diane spoke of.
We say it with those we love.
We say it looking
at who we are.
We say it clearly. We say it with words.
We say NO to this
repeat pattern built of colonisation
and slavery.

# A Short History of Mythology

*Jane Yeh*

To be a lady centaur
leaping across the Hedgehog Isles
Is to be in heaven
and wearing a tropical lei
Like a shower of spiral curls
my tail is springy
It smells like violets and shit
in a good way
Thank you pool
I can bounce down a peninsula
Laden with Gorgonzola
harvesting bites between watching
my shows
And inventing the handsaw
between weaving a tapestry
And visiting space
I will stomp on a few thousand years
Of lady centaur history
without regrets
To leap through a waterfall
in a novelty T-shirt
Holding a gift basket between my teeth
to shake my legs around
Pretending to be a freaky spider
to investigate a mole all day

Or whatever is stealing my tomatoes

is a paradise

Like a partridge

my head bobs when I run

My boobs bob when I run

when I run into the purple

tinged hills

I can be mythical

like the very specific flower

They use in salads in LA

as a garnish

If you look at it upside down

you can see the face of a furious

boy

# ritual purifcation of land and water

*Flora Yin Wong*

As a representation
of Good and of Evil,
It is said to be about the equalisation, of a balance,
Not to strive for the riddance of one or the other,
Rangda, the witch, and Barong the four-legged animal.

In a trance ritual of
fire,
rope,                nails

Men, women, and children attack themselves with daggers,
Eat glass, or walk on coals,
Convulsing violently in rigid shapes and forms,
A state of true absorption,
Tears are proof a supernatural force is near.

A bodily offering, dispelling violent and emotional desires,
Eyes wide, moving side to side, and back to
centre,

Canine teeth fled down to eradicate animal nature,
They are awakened and cleansed with holy water.

Hearing many voices,
Foreign spirits overtake the dancers,

Warding the body from physical
harm,
Young girls are transformed into part god,
Given the power to control effigies. 'Smoke from the mountain',
Land is maintained by the gods,
In one year,
Everything that happened today, Will happen again.

# Afterword
# Two of Swords

## *Sarah Shin*

Act 1

*Dream – the last glance just before waking. A euphonious alphabet climbs over a rock.*

S: It was autumn, the best of it: bright and fresh. Karma was a place on Packington Street. I remember thinking I would remember this moment again in the next world.

S: You were listening to a song on repeat. *Tear myself apart from this/ Break a hole inside the day.*

S: The first venture, the first sky.

Act 2

*A green dome within the ubiquitous green. The vegetal being opens like a flower to show its body, a sign that spells 'love'.*

S: Often, there's no sound when people speak to me in my dreams.

S: A silent alarm.

S: We were driving, the monster and I, to the bell cemetery. Huge bells, decommissioned and lying on their side.

S: The sense of waiting. *[To us]* What else?

S: A difficult cut.

## Act 3

*Backstage of the theatre, the room contains a box: the cipher of ciphers.*

S: Who is this dreaming 'I'? Who is this self to whom I've been so attached?

S: The Two of Swords is death in life, the snake that eats its tail.

*S casts a circle around them.*

S *[to us]*: Here, I meet the old woman, who cuts a hole in my chest and hides some earth in me.

S pushes a small knife into S. She opens up the wound and puts a handful of soil into it. The circle falls away.

S *[to us]*: When I wake up, the wound is healing, and she says that it is necessary, sometimes, to grieve the loss of illusions.

S: Why do we recoil at the sight of woundedness? The oracle spoke about the power of utterance. Every no is an affirmation, to break the code.

S: Death is the awakening that 'happens to you'. Eternity is always being awake.

S: Speak your dreams into this sleep of our life: so you remember it, when you wake up in the unwinding.

END

# Contributors

**Kaveh Akbar** is the founding editor of *Divedapper*. His poems have appeared in *The New Yorker, Poetry, Tin House, Ploughshares* and elsewhere. The recipient of a 2016 Ruth Lilly and Dorothy Sargent Rosenberg Fellowship from the Poetry Foundation and the Lucille Medwick Memorial Award from the Poetry Society of America, Akbar was born in Tehran, Iran, and currently lives and teaches in Florida.

**Rachael Allen** was born in Cornwall and studied English Literature at Goldsmiths College. She is the poetry editor at *Granta* and co-editor at the poetry press Clinic and the online journal *Tender*. A pamphlet of her poems was published as part of Faber New Poets and her first collection will be published by Faber in 2019. She is the recipient of an Eric Gregory award and New Writing North's Andrew Waterhouse award.

**Nuar Alsadir** is a poet, essayist and psychoanalyst. She is the author of the poetry collections *Fourth Person Singular* (2017), a finalist for the 2017 National Book Critics Circle Award for Poetry and shortlisted for the 2017 Forward Prize for Best Collection; and *More Shadow Than Bird* (Salt Publishing, 2012). She is a fellow at The New York Institute for the Humanities and works as a psychotherapist and psychoanalyst in private practice in New York.

**Khairani Barokka** is a writer, poet, and artist from Jakarta. Her work centers disability justice as anti-colonial praxis and access as translation. Okka was shortlisted for the 2023 Asian Women of Achievement Awards, and her latest books are 2022's *Ultimatum Orangutan*, which was shortlisted for the Barbellion Prize, and 2024's *amuk*, both published by Nine Arches.

**Emily Berry** has published two books of poems, *Dear Boy* (Faber, 2013) and *Stranger, Baby* (Faber, 2017). She edits *The Poetry Review* and is a fellow of the Royal Society of Literature.

**A. K. Blakemore** was born in London in 1991. Twice named a Foyle Young Poet of the Year, her work has been widely published and anthologised, appearing in journals including *Poetry London*, *Poetry Review* and *Ambit*. Her debut collection, *Humbert Summer*, appeared in 2015 and was awarded the Melita Hume Prize. *Fondue* was published by Offord Road Books in July 2018.

**Anthony V. Capildeo** FRSL is a Trinidadian Scottish poet and writer of non-fiction, whose interests include plurilingualism, silence, memory, place, ecopoetics, and traditional masquerade. Writer in Residence and Professor at the University of York, Capildeo's work has been recognised with awards such as the Forward Poetry Prize for Best Collection (*Measures of Expatriation*, 2016). Their ninth full-length collection, *Polkadot Wounds* (Carcanet, 2024) crystallised in Launceston, Cornwall, at Cyprus Well, the former home of Charles Causley, thanks to the Charles Causley Trust.

**Jen Calleja** is a writer and literary translator from German. Her debut poetry collection *Serious Justice* (2016) was published by Test Centre. She has translated literary fiction and non-fiction by many contemporary authors and figures including Wim Wenders, Kerstin Hensel and Gregor Hens. She lives in London.

**Dr Elinor Cleghorn** is a writer working across feminist visual cultures, histories of medicine, and narrative poetry. Her critical scholarship has been published in journals including *'Screen'*, *The Moving Image Review* and *Art Journal*. She was shortlisted for the Fitzcarraldo Editions essay prize 2017, and is currently writing a research memoir about autoimmunity. Her debut poetry pamphlet, *lupercalia*, was published by Litmus Press last year. Elinor can be found at www.theunwellwoman.com

**CAConrad** is the author of nine books of poetry and essays. *While Standing in Line for Death* (Wave Books), received the 2018 Lambda Award. A recipient of a Pew Fellowship in the Arts, they also received The Believer Magazine Book Award and The Gil Ott Book Award. They teach regularly at Sandberg Art Institute in Amsterdam, and their books, essays, films, interviews, rituals and other publications can be found online at http://CAConrad.blogspot.com

**Nia Davies** was born in Sheffield and studied English at the University of Sussex. She has been editor of *Poetry Wales* since 2014. Her pamphlets, *Then Spree* (Salt, 2012), *Çekoslovakyalıla tıramadıklarımızdanmısınız or Long Words* (Boiled String, 2016) and *England* (Crater, 2017), were followed by her first book-length collection, *All fours* (Bloodaxe Books, 2017), shortlisted for the Roland Mathias Poetry Award 2018 (Wales Book of the Year Awards). *Interversions* (Poetrywala, 2018) documents a collaboration with Kannada poet Mamta Sagar and *Key Blank* is out from the Literary Pocket Book series.

**Paige Emery** is an artist, herbalist, and plant dreamer exploring rituals of remembering the Earth. Her work is interested in interweaving rituals and critical ecology, ancestral memory and embodied futurities, ecopoetics and environmental praxis. This takes shape through multitudes of entangled forms such as paintings alchemised with plants, land-based art installations, ecopoetics and plant rituals, performance lectures, ecology walks and herbal remedies.

**Livia Franchini** is a writer and translator from Tuscany, Italy. She is the author of a novel, *Shelf Life* (Doubleday, 2019) and a poetry pamphlet, *Our Available Magic* (Makina Books, 2019). She is Lecturer in Creative Writing at Goldsmiths, where she also coordinates The Goldsmiths Prize. With Lucy Mercer, she co-edits *TOO LITTLE/TOO HARD*, a magazine on the intersections of work, time and value. She lives in London.

**Alexis Pauline Gumbs** is the author of *Undrowned: Black Feminist Lessons from Marine Mammals, Dub: Finding Ceremony, M Archive: After the End of the World* and *Spill: Scenes of Black Feminist Fugitivity*, and co-editor of *Revolutionary Mothering: Love on the Frontlines*. In 2020, she was awarded the National Humanities Center Fellowship for her book *Survival Is a Promise: The Eternal Life of Audre Lorde*.

**Will Harris** is the author of *RENDANG* (2020) and *Brother Poem* (2023), both published by Granta in the UK and Wesleyan University Press in the US.

**Caspar Heinemann** is an artist and writer living in Glasgow. He has had solo exhibitions at Édouard Montassut, Paris (2023); Cabinet, London (2022); Cell Project Space, London (2019); Outpost Gallery, Norwich (2017); Almanac, London (2017); and Kevin Space, Vienna (2016). Group exhibitions include Morena di Luna – Maureen Paley, Hove (2024); Casa di Goethe, Rome (2024); EACC, Castellón (2023); ICA, Los Angeles (2022); ICA, London (2019). His first poetry collection, *Novelty Theory*, was published in 2019 by The 87 Press. He is a postgraduate researcher in Theology and Literature at the University of Glasgow.

**Lucy Ives** is the author of *Life Is Everywhere: A Novel* and, most recently, *An Image of My Name Enters America: Essays*, both published by Graywolf Press. She teaches at Brown University and is currently writing a book about a literary phenomenon she terms the 'weak novel'.

**Rebecca May Johnson** is a writer and literary curator living in London. Her writing has appeared in the *TLS, LRB blog, The Financial Times, Guardian, Vogue* and many other publications. She is co-founder and curator of 'Voices at The Table' and co-curates 'Sitting Room', a long-running series of readings. She created the Food Memory Bank, a digital project to collect public memory about food and eating. Rebecca recently completed a PhD about a contemporary feminist reworking of

*The Odyssey* at UCL and works as researcher into literature and translation at Newcastle University. She is writing a book of public philosophy that takes food as its tool to think with.

**Bhanu Kapil** FRSL is the author of six full-length collections: *The Vertical Interrogation of Strangers* (Kelsey Street Press, 2001), *Incubation: a space for monsters* (Leon Works, 2006), *humanimal [a project for future children]* (Kelsey Street Press, 2009), *Schizophrene* (Nightboat, 2011), *Ban en Banlieue* (Nightboat, 2015), and *How to Wash a Heart* (Liverpool University Press, 2020). A new UK edition of *Incubation* (out of print for seven years in the US) was published by Prototype in 2023. A non-identical US version was published in the same year by Kelsey Street Press. Kapil is based now in Cambridge, where she is an Extraordinary Fellow of Churchill College. She has been awarded a Cholmondeley Award, a Windham-Campbell Prize and the T.S. Eliot Prize. For twenty years, she taught seminars in experimental writing, performance, and ritual at Naropa University. Currently, she is writing on impasse.

**Amy Key** is a writer based in London. She is the author of *Arrangements in Blue* (Jonathan Cape, 2023), chosen as a Book of the Year by the *Sunday Times, Independent, Irish Times* and *Granta* and shortlisted by Foyles for their Non-Fiction Book of the Year 2023. She is also the author of two collections of poetry, *Luxe* (Salt, 2013) and *Isn't Forever* (Bloodaxe, 2018). Her poems have been widely published and anthologised, and her essays have appeared in the collections *At The Pond* (2019) and *By the River* (2024) published by Daunt, as well as *Granta, Vogue*, the *Poetry Review* and elsewhere.

**Daisy Lafarge** lives in Glasgow. She is the author of a novel, *Paul* (Granta 2021), which won a Betty Trask Award and was a *New York Times* Editor's Choice, and a poetry collection, *Life without Air* (Granta 2020), which was shortlisted for the T.S. Eliot Prize. *Lovebug*, a short book on the poetics of infection, was published by Peninsula Press in 2023.

**Dorothea Lasky** is the author of eight books of poetry and prose, including the forthcoming *MEMORY* (Semiotext(e)) and *The Shining* (Wave Books).

**Ursula K. Le Guin** was one of the finest writers of our time. Her books have won millions of devoted readers as well as many awards, including the National Book Award, the Hugo and Nebula Awards and a Newbery Honor. Among her novels, *The Left Hand of Darkness*, *The Dispossessed* and the six Earthsea books are undisputed classics. Her series Annals of the Western Shore won the PEN Center USA Children's Literature Award. In 2014 Le Guin was awarded the National Book Foundation Medal for Distinguished Contribution to American Letters. She lived in Portland, Oregon, until her death in January 2018.

**Francesca Lissette** was born on the outskirts of London in 1987. Xir first book *Teens* was published by Mountain Press (2012); Lisette's second book, *sub-rosa, or, The Book of Metaphysics* is forthcoming from Boiler House Press in 2018. Xir solo performance piece *TO MAKE MANIFEST: AN UNDOING* was presented at KN Raum für Kunst (Berlin) in 2017. Lisette offers creative spiritual counselling through astrology, tarot, somatics and ritual, as the Glitter Oracle.

**Canisia Lubrin** is a writer, editor and teacher, author of five books, including *The Dyzgraphxst* and *The World After Rain* (M&S, 2025). Her work has received a 2021 Windham-Campbell Prize, the OCM Bocas Prize for Caribbean Literature and Griffin Poetry Prize, among others. Lubrin has held fellowships at the Banff Centre, Civitella Ranieri, Literature Colloquium and several universities. She is Assistant Professor and coordinator of the University of Guelph Creative Writing MFA in the School of English and Theatre Studies, and poetry editor at McClelland & Stewart. *Code Noir* (Knopf, 2024) her fiction debut, contains fifty-nine drawings by acclaimed visual artist, Torkwase Dyson.

**So Mayer** is a writer and activist. Recent works include *Political Animals: The New Feminist Cinema* (IB Tauris), *(O)* (Arc) and *<jacked a kaddish>* (Litmus). They work with queer feminist film curation collective Club des Femmes. @troublemayer

**Karen McCarthy Woolf** was born in London to an English mother and a Jamaican father. She is the recipient of a Glenna Luschei/Prairie Schooner editors' award and holds a doctorate from Royal Holloway, University of London for her research into diversifying ecocritical discourse and new ways of writing about nature, the city and the sacred. Her celebrated début *An Aviary of Small Birds* was shortlisted for the 2015 Felix Dennis Prize for Best First Collection and the Fenton Aldeburgh First Collection Prize, as well as being a *Guardian* Book of the Year and a Poetry Book Society Recommendation. Her latest collection *Seasonal Disturbances* (2017) is a PBS Recommendation. Karen is the editor of several literary anthologies, most recently *Ten: Poets of the New Generation* (Bloodaxe, 2017).

**Lucy Mercer's** poems have been published in *Poetry Review, Poetry London* and *The White Review* amongst others. In 2017 she was the winner of the inaugural White Review Poet's Prize. She is studying for a PhD in 'Speculative Emblematics'.

Born in the lower Mekong Delta and raised in the Washington DC area, **Hoa Nguyen** is a poet and educator at Toronto Metropolitan University. Her books include *Red Juice*, the Griffin Prize-nominated *Violet Energy Ingots* and *A Thousand Times You Lose Your Treasure*, a finalist for the National Book Award and the General Governor's Literary Award. She's the 2024 recipient of the C.D. Wright Award in Poetry from the Foundation of Contemporary Art, an Aquarius and a Fire Horse.

**Precious Okoyomon** is a poet, chef and artist living in New York City. They make portals into new worlds. Okoyomon has had institutional solo exhibitions at the Luma Westbau in Zurich (2018) and at the MMK in Frankfurt (2020), major performances commissioned by the Serpentine Galleries, London (2019) and the Institute of Contemporary Art, London (2019), and was an artist-in-residence at Luma Arles (2020). Okoyomon's second book, *But Did You Die?*, was published by The Serpentine Galleries/Wonder Press in 2024.

**Rebecca Perry** has written two full-length poetry collections – *Beauty/Beauty* and *Stone Fruit* – both published by Bloodaxe Books (2015, 2021), as well as four pamphlets. Her poetry has been shortlisted for awards including the T.S. Eliot Prize and her first collection won the Michael Murphy Memorial Prize. Her first work of creative non-fiction – *On Trampolining* – was published by Makina Books in 2023.

**Nat Raha** is a poet and trans / queer activist, living in Edinburgh, Scotland. She is the author of numerous pamphlets and three collections of poetry: *of sirens / body & faultlines* (Boiler House Press, forthcoming), *countersonnets* (Contraband Books, 2013), and *Octet* (Veer Books, 2010). She is currently completing a PhD in queer Marxism and contemporary poetry at the University of Sussex. In 2017, Nat's essay 'Transfeminine Brokenness, Radical Transfeminism' appeared in the South Atlantic Quarterly, and she is the co-editor of *Radical Transfeminism* zine.

**Nisha Ramayya** is a poet and lecturer in Creative Writing at Queen Mary, University of London. Her pamphlets *Notes on Sanskrit* (2015) and *Correspondences* (2016) are published by Oystercatcher Press. *Threads*, a creative-critical pamphlet co-authored with Sandeep Parmar and Bhanu Kapil, is published by clinic. She is a member of the 'Race & Poetry & Poetics in the UK' research group and the interdisciplinary practice-as-research group Generative Constraints.

**Ariana Reines** is the author of *The Cow* (Alberta Prize 2006), *Coeur de Lion* (2007), *Mercury* (2011), & *A Sand Book* (forthcoming 2019 from Tin House). Her Obie-winning play *TELEPHONE* was commissioned by The Foundry Theatre in 2009 & published in 2018 by Wonder. She has created performances for The Whitney Museum of American Art, Swiss Institute, Stuart Shave/Modern Art, the Solomon R. Guggenheim Museum, & many others, & performs & teaches around the world. A Visiting Critic at Yale, she astrologizes at lazyeyehaver.com.

**Sophie Robinson** is a poet. She lives between London and Norwich, where she teaches Creative Writing at the University of East Anglia. Her new book *Rabbit* is forthcoming from Boiler House Press in November 2018.

**Erica Scourti** is an artist and writer, based in Athens and London. They have presented work internationally, at High Line New York, Wellcome Collection, Serendicity Festival, Hong Kong, Kunsthalle Wien, Hayward Gallery, Munich Kunstverein, ICA London, Athens Biennale: ECLIPSE (2021) and Survival Kit 13, Latvian Centre for Contemporary Art (2022). Their solo show Profiles of You, at EMST, the National Museum of Contemporary Art, Athens ran from Jan – May 2023. Their writing has been published in *On Care* (Ma Biblioteque, 2020) *Spells* (Ignota, 2018) and *Fiction as Method* (Sternberg, 2017) among others, and they guest-edited the *Happy Hypocrite: Silver Bandage* journal (2019). Their first poetry pamphlet, *NO TO SELF*, is out with Veer2 now. They are undertaking a PhD in Goldsmiths' Art Department, and are a Lecturer in BA Fine Art at Central St Martins.

**Tai Shani**'s artistic practice, comprising performance, film, photography and installation, uses experimental writing as a guiding method. Oscillating between theoretical concepts and visceral details, Shani's texts attempt to create poetic coordinates in order to cultivate fragmentary cosmologies of marginalised nonsovereignty. Shani is the joint 2019 Turner Prize winner together with Lawrence Abu Hamdan, Helen Cammock and Oscar Murillo. Her work has been shown extensively in Britain and internationally.

**Sarah Shin** is a writer, publisher, researcher and curator interested in transformation, mysticism, cosmic speculation and altered states. Her collaborations include *Mirror*, a video game that journeys through a mythical world of correspondences, created with the artist Sammy Lee. She is a founder of Silver Press, the feminist publisher, and Spiral House, a new imprint for art, poetry and ways of knowing; Ignota, a creative publishing and curatorial house that closed in 2024; New Suns literary festival at the Barbican Centre; and Standard Deviation, a multidisciplinary collective exploring the coincidence of psychic, geometric and inhabited spaces.

**Himali Singh Soin** is a writer and artist based between London and Delhi. She uses metaphors from outer space and the natural environment to construct imaginary cosmologies of interferences and entanglements. In doing this, she thinks through ecological loss and the loss of home, seeking shelter somewhere in the radicality of love. She has shown at Serpentine, Whitechapel and Mimosa House, London; TBA21, Madrid; Khoj, Delhi; Venice Biennale and Dhaka Art Summit among others. Her recent solo at The Art Institute of Chicago was an exploration of transnational nuclear culture. Her current research with her collective Hylozoic/Desires focuses on the metaphysics of salt, which began at DesertX in California last year and will continue in 2025 at Tate Britain and Somerset House in London.

**Rebecca Tamás** is the author of the poetry collection *WITCH* (Penned in the Margins, 2019), and the essay collection *Strangers: Essays* on the *Human and Nonhuman* (Makina Books, 2020), which was longlisted for the Rathbones Folio Prize 2021. Her second collection of poetry is forthcoming with Fitzcarraldo Editions. She is a Lecturer in Creative Writing at City St Georges, University of London.

**Bones Tan Jones** is a London-based artist, musician and performer. Bones's work is a spiritual practice that seeks to present an alternative, queer, optimistic dystopia. They work through ritual, meditating through craft, dancing through the veil betwixt nature and the other. Bones weaves a mycelial web of diverse, eco-conscious narratives which aim to connect, enthral and induce audiences to think more sustainably and ethically. Traversing pop music, sculpture, alter-egos, digital images and video work, Bones sanctifies these mediums as tools in their craft.

**Dolly Turing** is sometimes Dolly Dollycore and experiments with poetry, sound and movement to create rituals. Their current growing, evolving work *Quest(ion)* is a poetic ritual about places, movement, connections, attachment, interruption, otherworlds, wide open space, spirits, stories and nothingness. She has had work published by *Datableed*, *The Winter Olympiks* and *Litmus*.

**Jane Yeh** was born in America and has lived in London since 2002. She holds degrees from Harvard, Iowa, Manchester Metropolitan, and Royal Holloway London universities. Her first collection of poems, *Marabou* (Carcanet, 2005), was shortlisted for the Whitbread, Forward, and Aldeburgh poetry prizes. She was named a Next Generation poet by the Poetry Book Society for her second collection, *The Ninjas* (Carcanet, 2012). Her third collection, *Discipline*, is forthcoming from Carcanet in 2019.

**Flora Yin Wong** is an artist, writer and founder of the record label and publisher, Doyenne Books, releasing anthologies, tapes, pewter castings and one-off ephemera. Her first book *Liturgy*, exploring the lines between fiction and non-fiction was published in 2021 on PAN x Primary Information, whilst her debut album, *Holy Palm*, was released on Modern Love. As a musician she has performed at the likes of INA GRM, Palais de Tokyo, The ICA, MACRO Roma, MMCA Seoul, Fondation Beyeler Basel, FOG Triennale Milano, Volksbühne Theatre, Somerset House, The V&A Museum, Atonal Berlin, Unsound Festival, MUTEK Peru, Buenos Aires, and Montreal, New York's ISSUE Project Room, WWWB Tokyo, SOTO Kyoto etc.

'Prayer' by Kaveh Akbar, published in *Calling a Wolf a Wolf* (Alice James, 2017), is reproduced by permission of the author.

'Augury' by Nuar Alsadir, published in *More Shadow than Bird* (Salt, 2012), is reproduced by permission of the author and publisher.

'Canopy' by Emily Berry, published in *Stranger, Baby* (Faber & Faber, 2017), is reproduced by permission of the author and publisher.

'Camisado' by CAConrad, published in *The Scores*, is reproduced by permission of the author.

From 'The Hermit' by Lucy Ives, published in *The Hermit* (Song Cave, 2016), is reproduced by permission of the author.

'My Narrative Costume is a Witch Without Reputation' by Amy Key, published in *Isn't Forever* (Bloodaxe Books, 2018), is reproduced by permission of the author and publisher.

'Come to Dust' from *So Far So Good* is reproduced by kind permission of the estate of Ursula K Le Guin.

'If I Were A Buddhist I'd Chant for Your Happiness' by Karen McCarthy Woolf, published in *NW15: The Anthology of New Writing* edited by Bernardine Evaristo and Maggie Gee (Granta, 2007), is reproduced by permission of the author.

A version of 'Thursday' by Ariana Reines was published in *Spork* (2012) and is reproduced by permission of the author.

Published in 2025 by Spiral House, an imprint of Silver Press.

First published in this single edition in 2018 by Ignota (2018-2024), a press created by Sarah Shin and Ben Vickers. An archive of Ignota's works can be found at ignota.org.



1 2 3 4 5 6 7 8 9 10

ISBN-13: 978-1-7393717-3-9

Design by Rose Nordin
Illustration by Soraya Gilanni
Typeset in Electra by Alice Spawls
Printed and bound in Great Britain by CPI Group (UK) Ltd, Croydon CR0 4YY